A SELECTIVE CHECKLIST
OF THE PUBLISHED WORK
OF

Aubrey Beardsley

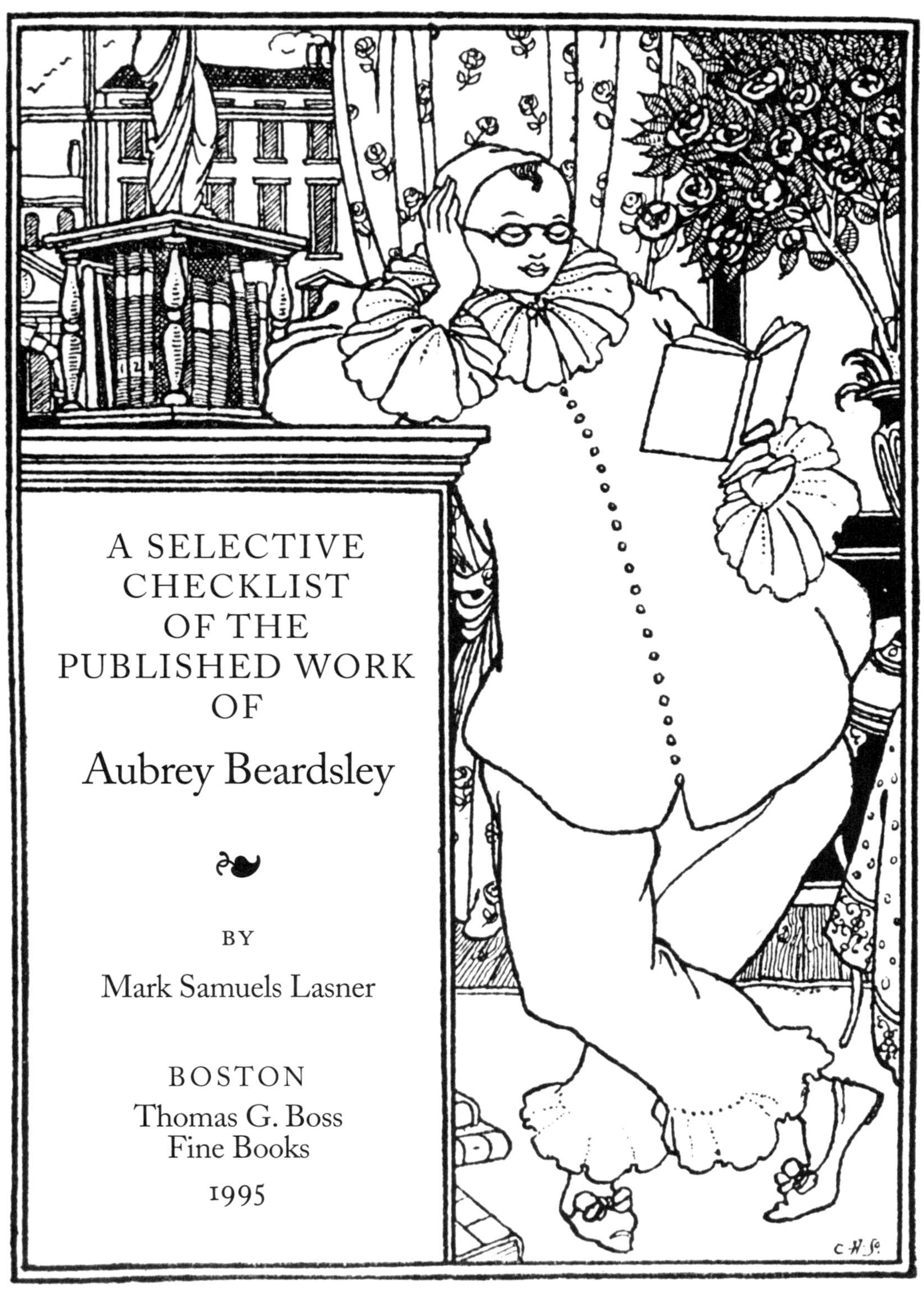

A SELECTIVE
CHECKLIST
OF THE
PUBLISHED WORK
OF

Aubrey Beardsley

BY

Mark Samuels Lasner

BOSTON
Thomas G. Boss
Fine Books
1995

PUBLISHED BY
Thomas G. Boss Fine Books
355 Boylston Street, Boston, Massachusetts 02116

ISBN 0-9644734-0-2

Photography by Robert Four (pp. 28 and 59) and
David Hagen (pp. 3, 8, 27, and 60)

DEDICATED
To the memory of Geoffrey Perkins

PRINTED BY THE STINEHOUR PRESS
LUNENBURG, VERMONT

By Way of Preface

Few artists—and certainly no British artist, with the possible exception of William Blake—have had so much written about them as Aubrey Beardsley. From Joseph Pennell's praise in "A New Illustrator," published in the inaugural issue of *The Studio* in April 1893, through the fusillade aimed at *The Yellow Book*, the eulogies of Max Beerbohm, Robert Ross, and Arthur Symons, the turn-of-the-century listings of Aymer Vallance and A. E. Gallatin, R. A. Walker's series of miscellanies spanning the teens through the forties, the Victoria and Albert Museum catalogue of 1966 and Brian Reade's subsequent book, to the biographies by Stanley Weintraub and Miriam J. Benkovitz and the recent (and forthcoming) critical studies by Linda Zatlin, there is a seemingly endless Beardsley literature—to mention only items written in the English language. One result of this plethora of books, monographs, and articles, some of them disorganized, if not contradictory or confusing, is that there exists no single, decently indexed source of reasonably reliable information, the kind of guide a collector, a curator, or a bookseller would want to keep handy. This publication, small as it is, is an attempt to fill that need by clarifying long-standing ambiguities and inaccuracies. It lists, in generally chronological order, most of what the artist published during his lifetime. Posthumously issued items are listed also, usually when these represent the first publication of significant work by Beardsley. In all, the approach has been *selective*, not all-encompassing, emphasizing those printed items that, over the years, have come to be sought by collectors and enthusiasts—the original editions of books and periodicals containing Beardsley's illustrations, drawings, designs, bindings, and writings. Nicholas Salerno has published a massive annotated bibliography of criticism, and a detailed catalogue raisonné of the original drawings is under preparation by Linda Zatlin. This checklist is not meant to compete with such works of detection and scholarship.

There is much about Beardsley and his publications that remains unknown or uncertain. At times a lack of facts has been covered over by layers of myth and "tradition," in which misconceptions first put into print years ago have been repeated again and again without challenge. To make matters worse, Beardsley's principal publishers, John Lane and Leonard Smithers (particularly the latter), were not always truthful about the number of copies printed—or about other matters. The limitations stated in contemporary advertisements and in the actual books themselves cannot, therefore, always be trusted. Neither can we believe just about any statements regarding so-called Beardsley "proofs." These usually turn out to be later reproductions or plates cut from books, not preliminary pulls made for the use of the artist or engraver. Such appellations as "suppressed" and "withdrawn" are common in the Beardsley literature, both because of the presumed erotic nature of his art and because of the premiums they can elicit from purchasers. I have tried to avoid the use of these often misleading terms, along with subjective designations of "rarity." My goal has been to set out the facts as best I can, with only an occasional foray into imperfectly informed speculation, knowing that there will be omissions and errors. Corrections will be welcome.

Most of what will be found here has been "stolen" from the obvious places. Reade and Dickinson's catalogues for the exhibitions held in London and New York in 1966–67 were my primary references, along with Vallance's 1909 "List of Drawings," Gallatin's 1945 *Catalogue of Drawings and Bibliography,* and Alexander Wainwright's careful description of the superlative Gallatin collection at Princeton (1952). (None of these, however, has any sort of index.) Brian Reade's *Beardsley* (1967), which principally deals with the drawings, has proved essential, too. I have also been aided by the many booksellers' and auctioneers' catalogues devoted in whole or in part to Beardsley, emanating from, among others, the Anderson Galleries, Dulau & Co., Elkin Mathews, J. Stephan Lawrence, Frank Hollings, Thomas G. Boss, Maggs Bros., and, perhaps most importantly, the late Geoffrey Perkins, of Warrack and Perkins, whose *Catalogue Sixty: Aubrey Beardsley* (1985) was a landmark unequalled in my collecting career. Many people have helped bring this work to completion. First and foremost, I wish to thank Susan Waterman, my research assistant, who brought an eagle eye and a steel-trap mind to bear on what might otherwise have ended up a muddle. James G. Nelson, whose history of the Bodley Head, *The Early Nineties,* and subsequent work on Elkin Mathews have proved invaluable, kindly let me use material about the Chiswick Press from a then-unpublished article on Leonard Smithers. Linda Zatlin took time from her own research to provide information and encouragement. The staffs of libraries have been generous with their help, in particular Mark J. Farrell, William A. Joyce, and Alexander D. Wainwright at Princeton; George Dalziel, Jr., Thomas F. J. McGill, Jr., and Neal T. Turtell at the National Gallery of Art; and Kirsten Tanaka at the San Francisco Performing Arts Library and Museum. I am also grateful to Alan Anderson, Karl Beckson, Robert Booth, David Bromer, Richard H. Cady, Alan Clodd, Philip K. Cohen, James Davis, Scott H. Duvall, R. A. Gekoski, Thomas A. Goldwasser, Greg Grainger, Sue Hamburger, James Havranek, David J. Holmes, John O. Kirkpatrick, Joe McCormack, William S. Peterson, Anthony Rota, Barbara Ceizler Silver, Margaret D. Stetz, Miriam Stewart, Roger E. Stoddard, Paul Voorhees, Benjamin Watson, Gail S. Weinberg, Stanley Weintraub, and John Windle.

[6]

List of Abbreviations

Gallatin *also* G	A. E. Gallatin, *Aubrey Beardsley: Catalogue of Drawings and Bibliography*. New York: The Grolier Club, 1945. [checklist no. 186; references are made to both item and page numbers]
Letters	*The Letters of Aubrey Beardsley*, ed. Henry Maas, J. L. Duncan, and W. G. Good. Rutherford, N. J.: Fairleigh Dickinson University Press, [1970]. [checklist no. 201]
Mason *also* M	Stuart Mason [Christopher Sclater Millard], *Bibliography of Oscar Wilde*. London: T. Werner Laurie, [1914]. [checklist no. 159]
Nelson	James G. Nelson, *The Early Nineties: A View from the Bodley Head.* Cambridge: Harvard University Press, 1971.
Reade *also* R	Brian Reade, *Beardsley.* London: Studio Vista, [1967]. [checklist no. 198]
Reade and Dickinson *also* R & D	Brian Reade and Frank Dickinson, *Aubrey Beardsley Exhibition at the Victoria and Albert Museum.* [London: Her Majesty's Stationery Office], 1966. [checklist no. 196]
Vallance *also* V	Aymer Vallance, "List of Drawings by Aubrey Beardsley," in Robert Ross, *Aubrey Beardsley.* London: John Lane, 1909. [checklist no. 154]
W	Georges Derry [R. A. Walker], "The Book-Plates of Aubrey Beardsley," *The Bookplate Booklet*, October 1919. [checklist no. 167]
Warrack and Perkins	*Catalogue Sixty: Aubrey Beardsley.* Church Enstone, Oxfordshire: Warrack & Perkins, [1985]. [checklist no. 209]

Note: Readers are reminded that this is a checklist, not a definitive bibliography. Some details are lacking or incomplete for items I have been unable to examine, and no attempt has been made to include every reference to the existing Beardsley literature. In addition, for the sake of simplicity, transcriptions of title-pages, publishers' names, places of publication, and the like have been regularized and, in many cases, truncated. The phrase "checklist no." refers to cross-references within this work.

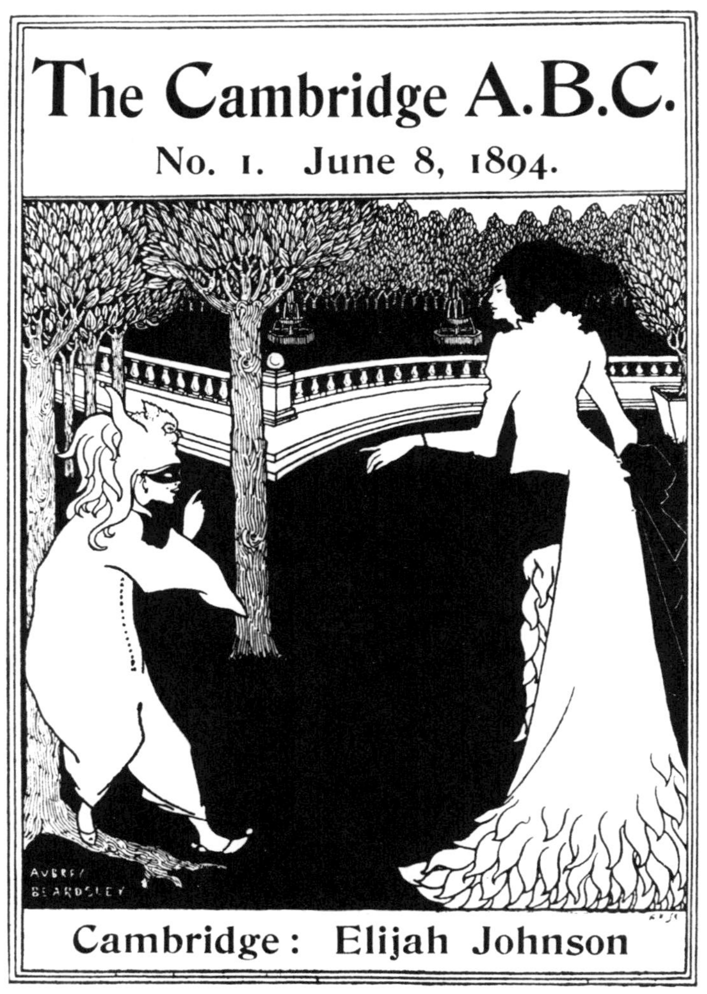

The Cambridge A.B.C. No. 1, 8 June 1894.
Cambridge: Elijah Johnson, 1894.
Front cover. [checklist no. 70]

[8]

1. PAST AND PRESENT. The magazine of the Brighton Grammar School. Vol. x, No. 2, June 1885.
By Beardsley: "The Valiant," poem written in 1885. The artist's first published literary work. Reprinted in Stanley Weintraub, *Beardsley,* checklist no. 199.
Wrappers. [G pp. 105–6; R & D 107]

2. PAST AND PRESENT. The magazine of the Brighton Grammar School. Vol. xii, No. 2, June 1887.
By Beardsley: "The Jubilee Cricket Analysis," series of 11 comic sketches on one sheet. The artist's first published drawings.
Grey wrappers. [G 101; R 8; R & D 109; V 9]

3. BRIGHTON SOCIETY. 9 July 1887.
By Beardsley: "A Ride on an Omnibus," poem signed "W. V. Beardsley." An extract was reprinted in *Reconsidering Aubrey Beardsley,* checklist no. 214.

4. BRIGHTON SOCIETY. 14 April 1888.
By Beardsley: "A Very Free (Library) Reading with Apologies to W. S. Gilbert," unsigned verse parody of William Schwenck Gilbert.

5. THE BRIGHTON GRAMMAR SCHOOL ANNUAL ENTERTAINMENT, AT THE DOME ON WEDNESDAY, DEC. 19, 1888. Programme & book of words. [Brighton: Tucknott's Steam Printing Works, 1888].[1]
By Beardsley: 11 illustrations (described as "Original Etchings by A. V. Beardsley, A Present Boy") to "The Pay of the Pied Piper: A Legend of Hamelin Town." Beardsley was in the cast of this comic opera by Fred Edmonds (words) and C. T. West (music) performed by the school; he also starred as Mercury in the prologue written by his schoolmaster, A. W. King.
Pink wrappers. [G 125–35, pp. 19–20; R 10; R & D 110; V 12]
Notes: Some copies of this program were issued (bound in) as a supplement to *Past and Present,* Vol. xiv, No. 1, February 1889. Five of the illustrations were reprinted in *The Westminster Gazette,* 25 March 1898, one in *The Magazine of Art,* May 1898, two in *The Poster,* August-September 1898, checklist no. 126, and one in the E. J. Marshall Memorial Number of *Past and Present,* December 1900, checklist no. 135.

[1] No issuer's name is given; the imprint is found on the last page of the book.

5A. THE PAY OF THE PIED PIPER. Reprinted from the 1888 Xmas Entertainment Programme of the Brighton Grammar School. [Brighton? 1898].
By Beardsley: 11 illustrations to "The Pay of the Pied Piper," reprinted from Brighton Grammar School *Programme & Book of Words,* checklist no. 5.
Loose plates in blue wrappers. [G p. 20]
Notes: R. A. Walker described this as a "special paper re-issue" in a manuscript note inserted in his copy.

6. TIT-BITS. Vol. XVII, No. 429, 4 January 1890.
By Beardsley: "The Story of a Confession Album," unsigned short story.[2] Reprinted in Linda Zatlin, "'The Story of a Confession Album': The Precursor of Aubrey Beardsley's Fascination with Triangles," *Transforming Genres: New Approaches to British Fiction of the 1890s,* ed. Nikki Lee Manos and Meri-Jane Rochelson (1994).
Self-wrappers. [G p. 106]

7. THE BEE. The magazine of Blackburn Technical School. [Blackburn, Lancashire], Vol. II, Part 2, November 1891.
By Beardsley: Frontispiece, "Hamlet Patris Manem Sequitur," reproduced as a lithograph printed in sanguine.[3]
Pale red-brown wrappers. [G 195; R 22; R & D 120, 124; V 31]

8. THE PALL MALL BUDGET. No. 1271, 2 February 1893.
By Beardsley: Five drawings: "Mr. H[enry]. A[rthur]. Jones and His Bauble" and "The New Coinage. (Designs that were not sent in for competition.)" depicting a girl seated on a sand castle, caricature in the style of Sir John Everett Millais; a caricature of Walter Crane's socialist opinions; a caricature of Britannia in the style of Sir Edward Burne-Jones; and a caricature of Whistler's "butterfly" signature.
Yellow wrappers. [G 248–52; R 38–40; R & D 158–60; V 55 1–11]

[2] Beardsley's juvenile writings included, apart from this story, a number of dramatic works. "A Brown Study," an unpublished farce, was performed at the Conversazione held at the Royal Pavilion, Brighton, for the Brighton Grammar School Old Boys' Association, on 7 November 1890. The programme (listing the cast members) is R & D 106. According to Charles B. Cochran (who performed in and produced the play and who later became a famous theatrical impresario), there was also a monologue titled "A Race for Wealth," apparently left incomplete after the first act. The manuscripts of this and of "A Brown Study," once in Cochran's possession, are now lost. See G p. 106.
[3] Reade states that "Beardsley's drawing was redrawn professionally on the lithographic stone for the frontispiece." An anonymous note (by A. W. King) titled "Our Illustrator," printed on pp. 21–22 of the issue, must be one of the earliest published comments on the artist.

9.   THE PALL MALL BUDGET. No. 1272, 9 February 1893.
By Beardsley: Ten drawings: "Mr. [Henry] Irving as Becket"; seven in article,
"'Becket' at the Lyceum" (caricatures of participants in Tennyson's *Becket*):
"Miss [Ellen] Terry," "Master Leo [Byrne]," "Queen Eleanor," "Margery"
[Kate Phillips], "The King Makes a Move on the Board" [William Terriss],
"Mr. [Edward] Gordon Craig," and "The Composer" [C. Villiers Stanford,
who wrote the music for the play]; one in article, "'Le Rêve'": "Emile Zola";
and one in article, "Comments on News": "The Disappointment of Emile
Zola."
Yellow wrappers.   [G 253–62; R 42–47; R & D 149–54, 157; V 55 III–IV]

9A. PICTURES OF 1893. [London: Pall Mall Gazette], 1893.
By Beardsley: "Emile Zola," reprinted from *The Pall Mall Budget,* checklist
no. 9. Reprinted in *The Studio,* Vol. 1, No. 3, June 1893.
Orange wrappers.   [V 55 IV]
Notes: Published 16 May 1893.

10.   THE PALL MALL BUDGET. No. 1273, 16 February 1893.
By Beardsley: Two drawings in article, "Verdi's 'Falstaff' at Milan": initial letter
"V" and "Giuseppe Verdi."
Yellow wrappers.   [G 263–64; V 55 V]

11.   THE PALL MALL BUDGET. No. 1274, 23 February 1893.
By Beardsley: Six drawings: two in article, "Leo the Thirteenth's Jubilee":
"The Pilgrim (Old Style)" and "The Pilgrim (New Style)," and four in arti-
cle, "The Reappearance of Mrs. Bancroft" (caricatures of participants in
Diplomacy by B. C. Stephenson and Clement Scott): "Mr. Arthur Cecil
(Baron Stein)," "Mrs. [Marie] Bancroft (Lady Fairfax)," "Mr. [Johnston]
Forbes Robertson (Julian Beauclerc)," and "Mr. [Squire] Bancroft (Count
Orloff)."
Yellow wrappers.   [G 265–70; R 48–50; R & D 155–56; V 55 VI–VII]

12.   THE PALL MALL BUDGET. No. 1276, 9 March 1893.
By Beardsley: Caricature of a golf player in classical helmet, illustrating the
poem fragment, "Aeneas on the Links." Reprinted in *The Early Work,* check-
list no. 133.
Yellow wrappers.   [G 271; V 55 VIII]
Notes: The poem is facetiously described as in the style of Alexander Pope.

13. THE PALL MALL BUDGET. No. 1277, 16 March 1893.
By Beardsley: Four drawings in review of Gluck's *Orpheus*, "A Royal College of Music Performance: 'Orpheus' at the Lyceum": "One of the Spirits (Act II)," "A Visitor at the Rehearsal" [Henry Irving], "Orpheus (Miss Clara Butt)," and "Some Dresses in the Chorus."
Yellow wrappers. [G 272–75; V 55 IX]

14. THE PALL MALL BUDGET. No. 1278, 23 March 1893.
By Beardsley: Portrait, "The Late Jules Ferry," in article, "M. Jules Ferry."
Yellow wrappers. [G 276; V 55 X]

15. THE PALL MALL BUDGET. No. 1279, 30 March 1893.
By Beardsley: "Bullet Proof Uniform: Tommy Atkins thinks it rather fun" in article, "Uniforms Absolutely Bullet-Proof."
Yellow wrappers. [G 277; R 51; V 55 XI]

16. THE STUDIO. Vol. I, No. I, April 1893.
By Beardsley: Front cover design, and nine drawings, six in article, "A New Illustrator: Aubrey Beardsley" by Joseph Pennell: three designs for *Le Morte Darthur*, "The Birthday of Madame Cigale," "Les Revenants de Musique," "J'ai Baisé Ta Bouche Jokanaan: Salomé with the Head of John the Baptist"; and three elsewhere in issue: "The Procession of Jeanne d'Arc" (pen-and-ink version), "Siegfried, Act II," and frieze from *Le Morte Darthur*.
Green wrappers. [G 200-1, 229–32, 851, and p. 88; R 164, 259–61; R&D 163, 362, 378–79; V 57]
Notes: There are perhaps three states of the front cover design. Reade and Dickinson comment: "The first state has no leaves to the right of the label STUDIO, is not bordered in black and lacks the label with the publisher's address at the bottom, besides other differences. The second state is similar to the poster but includes a figure of a faun with pipes sitting below the tree on the far left….the third state…[was] as it appeared on the wrapper [of *The Studio*]." Vallance changes the order, speaking only of "the original design containing a seated figure of Pan, omitted in the later version" printed on brown paper, the second state printed "black on green, also in gold on rough white paper for presentation to Royalty (Nov. 15th, 1893)."[4] At least two different designs were used for prospectuses and posters. A poster made from the third state, printed in light green, is described in R & D 379 and G 851.[5]

[4] Vallance 57 1. Gallatin 851 agrees with this order of precedence.
[5] In 1966 Anthony d'Offay issued a facsimile of this poster; see notes on the poster to advertise the Keynotes Series, checklist no. 47, and footnote 29, page 26.

16A. THE STUDIO. Vol. 1, No. 2, May 1893.
By Beardsley: "The Procession of Jeanne D'Arc" (pen-and-ink version), line block on folding supplementary plate, reprinted from *The Studio*, April 1893, checklist no. 16.
Green wrappers.   [G 201; V 57 VII]

17. THE PALL MALL BUDGET. No. 1282, 20 April 1893.
By Beardsley: "Mr. Frederick Harrison's 'Ideal Novelist'" (signed "Asmodeus") in article, "The Decadence of Romance."
Yellow wrappers.   [G 278; V 55 XII]

THE BON-MOTS SERIES

18. **Sydney Smith and R. Brinsley Sheridan**
BON-MOTS OF SYDNEY SMITH AND R. BRINSLEY SHERIDAN. Edited by Walter Jerrold. With grotesques by Aubrey Beardsley. London: J. M. Dent, 1893.
By Beardsley: 74 grotesques, title-page design, and front cover ornament—subsequently used for further volumes in the Bon-Mots Series, checklist nos. 19 and 20.
Cream cloth.   [G 642–771 and pp. 36–37; R 165–215; V 65]

ORDINARY ISSUE   [R & D 267, 272]

LARGE PAPER ISSUE   [R & D 268, 270]
100 numbered copies.

Notes: Published in June 1893. The Bon-Mots Series consisted of five volumes in all, the last two of which, *Bon-Mots of the Eighteenth Century* and *Bon-Mots of the Nineteenth Century* (both 1897), are illustrated by Alice B. Woodward but retain the front cover ornament by Beardsley.[6] According to Gallatin the ordinary copies were issued in a "light yellow-gray dust jacket, with design by Beardsley."

[6] Woodward, active in the period 1880–1920, was primarily known as an illustrator of children's books, among them Mrs. Molesworth's *The House That Grew* (1900), W. S. Gilbert's *The Pinafore Picture Book* (1908), and an undated edition of *Alice's Adventures in Wonderland.* According to Simon Houfe, *The Dictionary of British Book Illustrators and Caricaturists, 1880–1914* (1981), p. 504, "Her work was greatly admired by *The Studio*." Further impressions (designated as "editions" on title-pages) of some of the ordinary paper issues in the Bon-Mots Series were also published. Copies of an 1895 "Second Edition" of *Bon-Mots of Charles Lamb and Douglas Jerrold* and of an 1894 "Third Edition" of *Bon-Mots of Sydney Smith and R. Brinsley Sheridan* have been recorded.

19. **Charles Lamb and Douglas Jerrold**
BON-MOTS OF CHARLES LAMB AND DOUGLAS JER-
ROLD. Edited by Walter Jerrold. With grotesques by Aubrey Beardsley.
London: J. M. Dent, 1893.
By Beardsley: Grotesques (29 new designs, 39 reprinted from first Bon-Mots
Series volume, checklist no. 18, some repeated), title-page design, and front
cover ornament (also repeated from first Bon-Mots Series volume).
Cream cloth. [G 642–771 and pp. 36–37; R 216–31; V 65]

ORDINARY ISSUE [R & D 274]

LARGE PAPER ISSUE [R & D 271]
100 numbered copies.

Notes: Published in December 1893.

20. **Samuel Foote and Theodore Hook**
BON-MOTS OF SAMUEL FOOTE AND THEODORE
HOOK. Edited by Walter Jerrold. With grotesques by Aubrey Beardsley.
London: J. M. Dent, 1894.
By Beardsley: Grotesques (25 new designs, 41 reprinted from earlier Bon-
Mots Series volumes, checklist nos. 18 and 19, some repeated), title-page de-
sign, and front cover ornament (also repeated from earlier Bon-Mots Series
volumes).
Cream cloth. [G 642–771 and pp. 36–37; R 232–50; V 65]

ORDINARY ISSUE [R & D 273, 279]

LARGE PAPER ISSUE [R & D 269]
100 numbered copies.

Notes: Published in March 1894.

21. THE PALL MALL MAGAZINE. Vol. 1, No. 2, June 1893.
By Beardsley: "Of a Neophyte and how the Black Art was revealed unto him
by the Fiend Asomuel," illustration to "The Black Art: Part 11" by James
Mew.
Wrappers. [G 852; R 262; R & D 284; V 60 1]
Notes: "The artist invented the name Asomuel, meaning insomnia, for the
purpose of this illustration, which was a facetious comment on the article
that accompanied it."[7]

---

[7] Reade 262.

22. **Sir Thomas Malory**
THE BIRTH, LIFE, AND ACTS OF KING ARTHUR, OF
HIS NOBLE KNIGHTS OF THE ROUND TABLE, THEIR
MARVELLOUS ENQUESTS AND ADVENTURES, THE
ACHIEVING OF THE SAN GREAL, AND IN THE END,
LE MORTE DARTHUR WITH THE DOLOUROUS
DEATH AND DEPARTING OUT OF THIS WORLD OF
THEM ALL. The text as written by Sir Thomas Malory and imprinted
by William Caxton at Westminster the year MCCCCLXXXV, and now
spelled in modern style. With an introduction by Professor [John] Rhys, and
embellished with many original designs by Aubrey Beardsley. [London:
J. M. Dent], 1893–94.
By Beardsley: Front cover design, 16 full-page and four double-page illustra-
tions, 43 borders (some repeated), 288 chapter headings, initial letters, and
ornaments (many repeated).[8]   [G 284–627 and pp. 33–36; R 56–152;
R & D 164–97, 200–203, 216–22, 224–28, 231–32; V 59]

ORDINARY ISSUE   [R & D 205–8, 210–11]
12 parts issued at intervals beginning in June 1893. Green wrappers, inside
and outside back wrappers printed with advertisements for books published
by Dent and by Macmillan, respectively. Then bound in two vols.—by publisher or another binder—in cream cloth cases (with front cover, back cover
[publisher's device], and spine designs by Beardsley) supplied by Dent. 1,500
copies. A facsimile of the two-vol. version was published by Boydell, Woodbridge, Suffolk, in 1985.

SPECIAL ISSUE   [R & D 212–13]
12 parts, published at same intervals as ordinary issue but in grey wrappers
(inside and outside back wrappers also printed like ordinary issue). Then
bound in three vols.—by publisher or another binder—like ordinary issue in
cream cloth cases supplied by Dent; or, more commonly, in cream vellum—
with same designs as the clothbound copies—bound by the publisher. 300
numbered copies printed on Van Gelder paper (some copies not numbered).
The full-page plates are printed on French handmade etching paper, and the
two photogravure frontispieces are printed on mounted India paper. In addition, the publisher's device on the title-pages and 22 initials in the text are
rubricated.

---

[8] A. E. Gallatin and Alexander D. Wainwright, *The Gallatin Beardsley Collection in the Princeton
University Library,* checklist no. 193, p. 23. Gallatin p. 36 and *Letters* p. 278 note that four of the
Beardsley illustrations served as the (reduced-size photogravure) frontispieces to the Temple
Classics Series miniature edition of the work, published by Dent in four vols. in 1897.

Notes: The publishing history and bibliographical complexity of this work, commonly known—from the title printed on the wrappers—as *Le Morte Darthur* (or incorrectly as *Le Morte De Arthur* or *Le Morte D'Arthur*), can be treated here only in the broadest manner.[9] In the summer of 1892, probably in July, through the offices of F. H. Evans, the photographer and bookseller (Jones and Evans), Beardsley was introduced to the publisher J. M. Dent. Impressed by his drawings, including one entitled "Hail Mary"—and as a specialist in illustrated volumes well aware of the impact being made by William Morris's medievalistic Kelmscott Press books—Dent saw a remarkable opportunity in the twenty-year-old artist, considering him the potential illustrator of an already-contemplated edition of Malory. A sample drawing, "The Achieving of the Sangrael,"[10] met with the publisher's approval and Beardsley was commissioned with "everything to do for the book" for £200.[11] Beardsley began work on the designs in the fall of 1892, and the work was issued from June 1893 to November 1894 in 12 parts, in two types, an ordinary issue of 1,500 copies in green wrappers priced at 2*s.* 6*d.*, and a special or "superior" issue (sometimes wrongly termed "large paper" in booksellers' catalogues and even by the publisher)[12] of 300 numbered copies on Van Gelder paper in grey wrappers at 6*s.* 6*d.* The entire edition consisted of 1,800 copies. When, in 1894, the parts issue was due to be completed, subscribers were offered the opportunity to have their sets bound in binding-cases bearing new cover and spine designs by Beardsley.[13] According to a slip placed in Part XII, owners of both ordinary and special issue ("Large Paper") copies had the choice of buying cloth cases from Dent or sending their sets to Dent to be bound. Purchasers of the special issue who wanted their sets bound in the recommended vellum, however, *had* to send them to Dent.[14]

---

[9] More details, including collations of each part, descriptions of variations between the ordinary and special copies, and transcriptions of inserted slips, can be found in R. A. Walker, *Le Morte Darthur with Beardsley Illustrations*, checklist no. 188.

[10] Reade 33, ultimately used as the frontispiece for Vol. II of *Le Morte Darthur.*

[11] *Letters* p. 34. Beardsley gives the figure as £200 in a letter to E. J. Marshall; the payment was raised later to £250.

[12] The leaf size is virtually the same for both issues.

[13] The preliminary matter needed for the bound volume was included in Parts VI and XII of the parts issue: this included title-pages bearing a headpiece and publisher's device (repeated on the back covers of the bound copies) by Beardsley. A slip inserted in Part XII gave "Directions to Binder" to "Please cancel Contents and List of Illustrations given in Part VI., and substitute those given in Part XII., which must be bound in Volume I."

[14] Contrary to the dominant interpretation, there were not "300 copies bound in vellum" but 300 copies printed on Van Gelder paper, only a portion of which were bound in vellum. How large a portion it is impossible to determine; possibly only half the purchasers bothered to send them to Dent. Copies of the special issue bound (in three vols.) in the publisher's cloth cases are even less common, yet one was recently offered in John Windle, *List Twenty-Three* (1994), item 20.

The binding configuration was two volumes for the ordinary issue, and three volumes (because of the thickness of the paper) for the special issue. Copies bound by the publisher had the wrappers removed and included a silk ribbon place-marker in each volume. Variants among copies bound by others are legion, with illustrations out of order and with front and back wrappers from the parts version sometimes inserted in a most haphazard way. Ready-made clothbound sets of the ordinary issue were offered for sale for two guineas.[15]

22A. Prospectus for *Le Morte Darthur*. April 1893.
By Beardsley: Border design, chapter heading, initial letters "A" and (in red) "I," and headpiece (later used on title-pages).
Folded leaf (same paper as used for the ordinary issue of the book).
Notes: A sample full-page illustration, "Merlin Taketh the Child Arthur into His Keeping," is sometimes found inserted. Dent's announced limitation on last page of the superior issue ("slightly larger in size") to "250 copies for sale in England, 200 of which will be issued in parts, the remaining 50 being reserved for sale in volumes" was not adhered to.

22B. [SECOND EDITION]. [London: J. M. Dent], 1909.
By Beardsley: Ten additional chapter headings inadvertently omitted from the first edition.[16]
Green cloth.   [G p. 36; R 153–57; R & D 198–99, 214, 223]
Notes: Published in September 1909. 1,500 copies (1,000 for the United Kingdom, 500 for the U.S.). This is the first edition to be issued in one volume.[17] A facsimile was published by Dorset Press, New York, in 1990.

22C. [THIRD EDITION]. And a note on Aubrey Beardsley by Aymer Vallance. [London: J. M. Dent], 1927.
By Beardsley: One additional chapter heading inadvertently omitted from previous editions; also a sketch for an unused front wrapper design.
Black cloth, dust jacket.   [G p. 36; R 55, 158; R & D 209, 215, 229–30]
Notes: Published in November 1927. 1,600 copies. Has a note by R. A. Walker on the drawings omitted from the first edition. Copies for sale in the U.S. form an American issue bound in black cloth with E. P. Dutton's name on verso of title-page. A facsimile of the third edition was published by Harrison House, New York, in 1985.

---

[15] Walker could find no record of the price of vellum-bound copies of the special issue, "probably because all the 300 copies were subscribed."
[16] R. A. Walker, *Le Morte Darthur with Beardsley Illustrations*, checklist no. 188, pp. 10–11.
[17] Bertram Rota cat. 64, *Books at Bodley House* (1940), lists as item 830 a one-volume "Second Edition" of 1899, limited to 1,000 copies. This is almost certainly a "ghost" resulting from the typographical error of "1899" for the correct "1909."

22D. REPRODUCTIONS OF ELEVEN DESIGNS OMIT-
TED FROM THE FIRST EDITION OF LE MORTE DAR-
THUR ILLUSTRATED BY AUBREY BEARDSLEY AND
PUBLISHED IN MDCCCXCIII. Also those made for the cover of
the issue in parts and a facsimile print of the Merlin drawing. With a fore-
word by Aymer Vallance and a note on the omitted designs by Rainforth
Armitage Walker. London: J. M. Dent, 1927.
By Beardsley: 14 drawings, comprising the 11 chapter headings omitted from
the first edition (as found in checklist nos. 22B and 22C), an enlarged reproduction of "Merlin," a sketch for an unused front wrapper design (previously
reproduced in checklist no. 22C), and the front wrapper design as published.
Brown calf-backed vellum boards.   [G 631–41 and p. 36; R & D 227–30]
Notes: Published in November 1927. 300 numbered copies. Generally
known (from the half-title) as the "Morte Darthur Portfolio" and issued in
conjunction with the third edition, checklist no. 22C. Front cover reuses the
design for the cloth and vellum-bound versions of the first edition.

22E. [FOURTH EDITION]. With an introduction by John Rhys and a
note on Aubrey Beardsley by Aymer Vallance. [London:] J. M. Dent, 1972.
Black cloth.
Notes: Facsimile of third edition, checklist no. 22C. An American issue was
published the same year by St. Martin's Press, New York. In 1988 Dent published another facsimile (a self-styled "fifth edition") with a revised publisher's note by F. J. Martin Dent.

22F. BEARDSLEY'S ILLUSTRATIONS FOR LE MORTE
DARTHUR. Reproduced in facsimile from the Dent edition of 1893–94.
Arranged by Edmund V. Gillon, Jr. New York: Dover Publications, [1972].
By Beardsley: The complete set of illustrations, initials, and ornaments for the
1893–94 first edition, checklist no. 22, with sample pages and reproductions
of the cover design for the issue in wrappers and of the cloth binding.
White wrappers.
Notes: With introductory publisher's note. In Dover Pictorial Archive Series.

23.   THE PALL MALL MAGAZINE. Vol. 1, No. 3, July 1893.
By Beardsley: "The Kiss of Judas," illustration to "A Kiss of Judas" by X. L.
Wrappers.   [G 853; R 263; R & D 285, 295; V 60 11]

24.   **Frances Burney**
EVELINA. Or the history of a young lady's entrance into the world. Ed-
ited by R. Brimley Johnson. Illustrated by W. Cubitt Cooke. London: J. M.
Dent, 1893.

By Beardsley: Title-page, subsequently used for the ordinary issues of publisher's editions of Burney's *Cecilia*, checklist no. 24A, and de Staël's *Corinne*, checklist no. 24B.   [G 855; R 34–35; V 62 1]

ORDINARY ISSUE   [R & D 282]
By Beardsley: Front cover design (not found on large paper issue), subsequently used for the publisher's editions of Burney's *Cecilia*, checklist no. 24A, and for de Staël's *Corinne*, checklist no. 24B.
Two vols. Light green cloth (also buff cloth).

LARGE PAPER ISSUE   [R & D 283]
Two vols. Buff cloth. 200 numbered copies (150 for England, 50 for America—imported by Macmillan).

Notes: Published in July 1893. The original drawing for the title-page (with the letterpress pasted on) was offered for sale and reproduced in Sotheby's catalogue of *Illustrated and Private Press Books, Conjuring and Circus, Children's Books and Juvenilia, and Related Drawings*, 17–19 June 1987, pp. 78–79. Beardsley probably was also responsible for the spine design found on both the ordinary and large paper issues, later used for *Cecilia*, checklist no. 24A, and for *Corinne*, checklist no. 24B.

24A. Frances Burney

CECILIA. Or memoirs of an heiress. Edited by R. Brimley Johnson. Illustrated by W. Cubitt Cooke. London: J. M. Dent, 1893.
By Beardsley: Title-page, previously used for *Evelina*, checklist no. 24.

ORDINARY ISSUE
By Beardsley: Front cover design (not found on large paper issue), previously used for *Evelina*, checklist no. 24.
Three vols. Light green cloth.

LARGE PAPER ISSUE
Three vols. Buff cloth. 200 numbered copies (125 for England, 75 for America—imported by Macmillan).

Notes: Published in December 1893. Beardsley probably was also responsible for the spine design found on both the ordinary and large paper copies, previously used for *Evelina*, checklist no. 24.

24B. Madame de Staël [Anne Louise Germaine Staël-Holstein, Baroness de Staël, née Necker]

CORINNE. Or Italy. With an introduction by George Saintsbury. Illustrated by H. S. Greig. London: J. M. Dent, 1894.
By Beardsley: Title-page, previously used for *Evelina*, checklist no. 24, and for *Cecilia*, checklist no. 24A.

By Beardsley: Front cover design (not found on large paper issue), previously used for *Evelina,* checklist no. 24, and for *Cecilia,* checklist no. 24A. Two vols. Light green cloth.

LARGE PAPER ISSUE

Two vols. Buff cloth. 100 numbered copies (50 for England, 50 for America—imported by J. B. Lippincott).

Notes: Published in November 1894. Beardsley probably was also responsible for the spine design found on both the ordinary and large paper copies, previously used for *Evelina,* checklist no. 24, and for *Cecilia,* checklist no. 24A.

THE KEYNOTES SERIES

25. **George Egerton [Mary Chavelita Dunne]**
KEYNOTES. London: Elkin Mathews and John Lane, 1893.
By Beardsley: Front cover and title-page design (altered version for title-page)[18] and key monogram (found on back cover, spine, and verso of contents leaf). [G 796; R 295; V 69 1]

FIRST ISSUE [R & D 302]
Pink wrappers. 500 copies.

SECOND ISSUE [R & D 303]
Light green cloth. 600 copies.

Notes: The first 500 copies of the first edition were issued in pink wrappers; the rest of the impression of 1,100, bound in green cloth, formed the inaugural volume in the Keynotes Series of novels and short fiction.[19] A collection of stories (not a single work as is sometimes supposed), *Keynotes* was the author's first book, with both issues published on 2 December 1893.[20] The

---

[18] The design was also used for the poster to advertise the first ten volumes in the Keynotes Series, see checklist no. 47, and on both title-page and front cover of the German translation (by Dr. Udelbert von Hagen) of *Keynotes,* entitled *Grundtöne,* published by Eduard Moss, Zurich, in 1896.

[19] Nelson p. 287, no. 74 in his checklist. *Keynotes* was highly successful; some 6,071 copies (in five impressions, marked "editions" on verso of title-pages) were printed by the time of the dissolution of the Mathews and Lane partnership in midsummer 1894.

[20] Egerton herself, however, gave the month of publication as September 1893 in "A Keynote to Keynotes," the autobiographical account she contributed to John Gawsworth [Terence Fytton Armstrong], *Ten Contemporaries: Notes Toward Their Definitive Bibliography* (1932), p. 59. She was probably thinking of the contract for the book, which was dated 26 August 1893; see Nelson p. 100.

series—which eventually ran to 33 titles—was published by John Lane in London and (with three exceptions) by the Boston firm Roberts Brothers.[21]

There has always been some uncertainty regarding which Keynotes Series books bear work by Beardsley. While it appears definite that he produced the front cover and title-page designs for the first 21 volumes and also for Vol. XXIII, John Smith's *Platonic Affections* (1896), the ornamental "key" monograms remain a matter for debate.[22] Reade and Dickinson state that the keys on "15 of the volumes" are by Beardsley—but they do not say precisely which ones or whether, in the cases of George Egerton, Grant Allen, and Arthur Machen, the count includes the repeated use of the same design. The Keynotes Series prospectus, checklist no. 48, reproduces 18 keys (for 21 volumes)—possibly not all by Beardsley—while Brian Reade, in his 1967 *Beardsley*, checklist no. 198, reproduces 14 keys from the series, for a total of 17 volumes, plus the key for *The British Barbarians*, checklist no. 98, on two plates.[23] Only four of the keys appear in Beardsley's drawings for the covers and title-pages, and even these are not necessarily connected to the surrounding designs. Amid this confusion it seems best to take a conservative approach in attributing the key monograms.

26. **Florence Farr**
THE DANCING FAUN. London: Elkin Mathews and John Lane, 1894.
By Beardsley: Front cover and title-page design and key monogram (found on back cover, spine, and verso of prefatory note leaf). [G 797; R 296; V 69 11]

[21] The name of Roberts Brothers appears on the title-pages of the English editions they co-published, but the firm also issued true American editions, printed from different typesettings in a smaller format. Grant Allen's *The British Barbarians,* checklist no. 45, bears the joint imprint of John Lane and G. P. Putnam's Sons; the final volumes in the series, *God's Failures* by J. S. Fletcher and *Mere Sentiment* by A. J. Dawson (both 1897 and designed by Patten Wilson), were published on both sides of the Atlantic by John Lane, who had opened a New York office in 1896. George Egerton's translation of Ola Hansson's *Young Ofeg's Ditties,* checklist no. 84, though not part of the series, was issued in similar style, with cover and title-page designed by Beardsley. A volume announced as a forthcoming Keynotes title, Allan Monkhouse's *A Deliverance,* ultimately appeared (in 1898) in a different format. For more about what Michael Sadleir called "the most elegant fiction series of the nineteenth century" (*XIXth Century Fiction* [1951], Vol. II, p. 139), see Wendell V. Harris, "John Lane's Keynotes Series and the Fiction of the 1890s," *PMLA* (1968), pp. 1407–13, and the many relevant entries in Margaret D. Stetz and Mark Samuels Lasner, *England in the 1890s: Literary Publishing at the Bodley Head* (1990).
[22] Gallatin 818–39 declares Beardsley responsible for all the keys for these 22 volumes. Michael Sadleir, usually accurate in all matters dealing with 19th-century bibliography, surely erred when he wrote that "Each book [in the entire Keynotes Series] has, on the spine, a specially drawn Key, incorporating the author's initial, which Keys were all Beardsley's work" (*XIXth Century Fiction,* Vol. II, p. 139).
[23] Reade Pls. 311–12, listed and described in two groups, nos. 313–14.

Notes: Vol. II of the Keynotes Series. Published ca. 4 June 1894. 1,100 cop-ies.[24] Author's first book. The faun is a caricature of James McNeill Whistler.

27. **F[yodor]. Dostoievsky**
POOR FOLK. Translated from the Russian of F. Dostoievsky by Lena Milman. With an introduction by George Moore. London: Elkin Mathews and John Lane, 1894.
By Beardsley: Front cover and title-page design and key monogram (found on back cover, spine, and p. [v]).
Yellow cloth.   [G 798; R 297; R & D 336–37; V 69 III]
Notes: Vol. III of the Keynotes Series. Published 30 June 1894. 1,100 copies.[25]

28. **Francis Adams**
A CHILD OF THE AGE. London: John Lane, 1894.
By Beardsley: Front cover and title-page design.
Dark green cloth.   [G 799; R 298; R & D 340; V 69 IV]
Notes: Vol. IV of the Keynotes Series. Published in November 1894.

29. **Arthur Machen [Arthur Llewellyn Jones]**
THE GREAT GOD PAN AND THE INMOST LIGHT. Lon-don: John Lane, 1894.
By Beardsley: Front cover and title-page design and key monogram (found on back cover and spine).
Dark blue-grey cloth.   [G 800; R 299; R & D 317; V 69 v]
Notes: Vol. v of the Keynotes Series. Published in December 1894. A second impression (marked "Second Edition") appeared in 1895.

30. **George Egerton [Mary Chavelita Dunne]**
DISCORDS. London: John Lane, 1894.
By Beardsley: Front cover and title-page design and key monogram (found on back cover and spine).
Red cloth.   [G 801; R 301; V 69 VI]
Notes: Vol. VI of the Keynotes Series. Published 8 December 1894.[26]

---

[24] Nelson p. 288, no. 92 in his checklist.
[25] Nelson p. 289, no. 97 in his checklist.
[26] Reade and Dickinson 331 for the second impression.

31. **M[atthew]. P[hipps]. Shiel**
PRINCE ZALESKI. London: John Lane, 1895.
By Beardsley: Front cover and title-page design.
Purple cloth.   [G 802; R & D 333; V 69 VII]
Notes: Vol. VII of the Keynotes Series. Published in March 1895. Author's
first book.

32. **[Charles] Grant [Blairfindie] Allen**
THE WOMAN WHO DID. London: John Lane, 1895.
By Beardsley: Front cover and title-page design and key monogram (found on
back cover, spine, and verso of preface leaf).
Olive green cloth.   [G 803; V 69 VIII]
Notes: Vol. VIII of the Keynotes Series. Published in February 1895.[27]

33. **H[enry]. D[awson]. Lowry**
WOMEN'S TRAGEDIES. London: John Lane, 1895.
By Beardsley: Front cover and title-page design.
Blue cloth.   [G 804; R & D 338–39; V 69 IX]
Notes: Vol. IX of the Keynotes Series. Published in May 1895.

34. **Henry Harland**
GREY ROSES. London: John Lane, 1895.
By Beardsley: Front cover and title-page design and key monogram (found on
back cover, spine, and verso of contents leaf).
Grey cloth.   [G 805; R 302; R & D 335; V 69 X]
Notes: Vol. X of the Keynotes Series. Published in May 1895. Four of the sto-
ries in the book had previously appeared in *The Yellow Book.*

35. **H[enry]. B[rereton]. Marriott Watson**
AT THE FIRST CORNER AND OTHER STORIES. London:
John Lane, 1895.
By Beardsley: Front cover and title-page design.
Dark blue cloth.   [G 806; R 303; R & D 342; V 69 XI]
Notes: Vol. XI of the Keynotes Series. Published in May 1895.

36. **Ella D'Arcy**
MONOCHROMES. London: John Lane, 1895.
By Beardsley: Front cover and title-page design and key monogram (found on
back cover, spine, and verso of contents leaf).
Olive cloth.   [G 807; R 304; R & D 323; V 69 XII]

---

[27] For a later impression and an American edition, see R & D 328–29.

Notes: Vol. XII of the Keynotes Series. Published 25 May 1895. The author's first book, dedicated to "The Chief," i.e., Henry Harland, literary editor of *The Yellow Book.* D'Arcy served as the unpaid and unacknowledged assistant editor of the magazine from its inception through part of 1896.

37. **Evelyn Sharp**
AT THE RELTON ARMS. London: John Lane, 1895.
By Beardsley: Front cover and title-page design and key monogram (found on back cover, spine, and verso of title-page).
Brown cloth.   [G 808; R 305; R & D 341; V 69 XIII]
Notes: Vol. XIII of the Keynotes Series. Published 8 June 1895. Author's first book.

38. **Gertrude Dix**
THE GIRL FROM THE FARM. London: John Lane, 1895.
By Beardsley: Front cover and title-page design and key monogram (found on back cover, spine, and verso of title-page).
Brown cloth.   [G 809; R 306; R & D 343; V 69 XIV]
Notes: Vol. XIV of the Keynotes Series. Published 20 June 1895.

39. **Stanley V[ictor]. Makower**
THE MIRROR OF MUSIC. London: John Lane, 1895.
By Beardsley: Front cover and title-page design and key monogram (found on back cover, spine, and recto of preliminary leaf π4).
Dark green cloth.   [G 810; R 307; R & D 306, 308; V 69 XV]
Notes: Vol. XV of the Keynotes Series. Published in August 1895. The author's first independent book, preceded by *The Passing of a Mood* (1893), a volume of stories published under the initials "V., O., C.S." to which Makower, Oswald Sickert, and Arthur Cosslett Smith contributed.

40. **W[illiam]. Carlton Dawe**
YELLOW AND WHITE. London: John Lane, 1895.
By Beardsley: Front cover and title-page design and key monogram (found on back cover, spine, and verso of contents leaf).[28]
Ochre cloth.   [G 811; R 308; R & D 321; V 69 XVI]
Notes: Vol. XVI of the Keynotes Series. Published in August 1895.

[28] *Letters* p. 83. A different "key" was used for Dawe's second Keynotes volume, *Kakemonos* (1897), which had a front cover and title-page design by Patten Wilson.

41. **Fiona Macleod [William Sharp]**
THE MOUNTAIN LOVERS. London: John Lane, 1895.
By Beardsley: Front cover and title-page design and key monogram (found on back cover, spine, and recto of preliminary leaf $\pi 4$).
Turquoise blue cloth. [G 812; R 309; R & D 318, 320; V 69 XVII]
Notes: Vol. XVII of the Keynotes Series. Published in July 1895.

42. **Victoria Crosse [Annie Sophie "Vivian" Cory]**
THE WOMAN WHO DIDN'T. London: John Lane, 1895.
By Beardsley: Front cover and title-page design and key monogram (found on back cover, spine, and recto of preliminary leaf $\pi 4$).
Red cloth. [G 813; R & D 325; V 69 XVIII]
Notes: Vol. XVIII of the Keynotes Series. Published 22 August 1895. The original title, *Consummation,* was altered to *The Woman Who Didn't* to take advantage of the notoriety of Grant Allen's *The Woman Who Did,* checklist no. 32, an earlier Keynotes book, with which it had, in reality, no connection.

43. **Arthur Machen [Arthur Llewellyn Jones]**
THE THREE IMPOSTORS. Or the Transmutations. London: John Lane, 1895.
By Beardsley: Front cover and title-page design and key monogram (found on back cover, spine, and verso of contents leaf).
Dark blue-grey cloth. [G 815; R & D 324; V 69 XX]
Notes: Vol. XIX of the Keynotes Series. Published in November 1895.

44. **Netta Syrett**
NOBODY'S FAULT. London: John Lane, 1896.
By Beardsley: Front cover and title-page design and key monogram (found on back cover, spine, and recto of preliminary leaf $\pi 4$).
Dark blue cloth. [G 814; R 310; R & D 332; V 69 XIX]
Notes: Vol. XX of the Keynotes Series. Published in February 1896. Author's first book.

45. **[Charles] Grant [Blairfindie] Allen**
THE BRITISH BARBARIANS. A hill-top novel. London: John Lane, 1895.
By Beardsley: Front cover and title-page design and key monogram (found on back cover, spine, and verso of title-page).
Olive green cloth. [G 816; R 311; R & D 314; V 69 XXI]
Notes: Vol. XXI of the Keynotes Series. Published in November 1895. Beardsley also produced the designs for H. D. Traill's 1896 parody of this title, *The Barbarous Britishers,* checklist no. 98, also published by John Lane.

46. **John Smith**
PLATONIC AFFECTIONS. London: John Lane, 1896.
By Beardsley: Front cover and title-page design.
Blue-green cloth, dust jacket.   [G 817; R 312; R & D 309, 311; V 69 XXII]
Notes: Vol. XXIII of the Keynotes Series. Published in April 1896. The author's name may be a pseudonym.

47. Poster to advertise the Keynotes Series. [May? 1895].
By Beardsley: Design adapted from the title-page for the first volume in the series, George Egerton's *Keynotes,* checklist no. 25.
Color lithograph.   [R & D 300]
Notes: Lists the first ten titles. Two apparent "states" are recorded, one (presumed to be the earlier) without Beardsley's name printed, the other with it. In both, the name of the printer "FORBES CO." is found in the lower right corner. Reade and Dickinson comment that "Few examples of this poster seem to have survived." A reproduction—one of a set of ten facsimile Beardsley posters—was issued by Anthony d'Offay, the London art dealer (and one-time antiquarian bookseller), in 1966 in an edition of 100 copies; like the others, this can be distinguished from the original by the presence of a printed legend, "Reissued by Anthony d'Offay 8 Vigo St W1. Set No." (followed by a number written in manuscript), immediately below the image.[29]

48. KEYNOTES SERIES OF NOVELS AND SHORT STORIES. Twenty-one designs by Aubrey Beardsley. With press notices. London: John Lane, 1896.
By Beardsley: Front cover and title-page design, plus reproductions of 21 of his 22 front cover and title-page designs for the Keynotes Series.
Light green wrappers.   [G p. 43; R & D 301; V p. 84]
Notes: Prospectus for the Keynotes Series, also reproducing 18 key monograms and containing advertisements for the Pierrot's Library volumes with Beardsley designs and for Lane's line of 4s. 6d. novels. The back cover design, depicting the publisher's premises in Vigo Street, is by Edmund H. New.

[29] The nine other d'Offay facsimiles reproduce: the poster for *The Studio,* checklist no. 16; the Avenue Theatre poster announcing *A Comedy of Sighs,* checklist no. 62; Lane's poster to advertise *The Yellow Book,* checklist no. 65F (also the version issued by Copeland and Day); two versions (one without letterpress) of the poster to advertise Children's Books published by T. Fisher Unwin, checklist no. 75; the Pseudonym and Autonym Libraries poster, checklist no. 76; the poster to advertise *The Spinster's Scrip,* checklist no. 92; and the poster for *The Savoy,* checklist no. 103B. Examples of the d'Offay posters have been passed off as originals and at least one has been reproduced as such in a Beardsley exhibition catalogue.

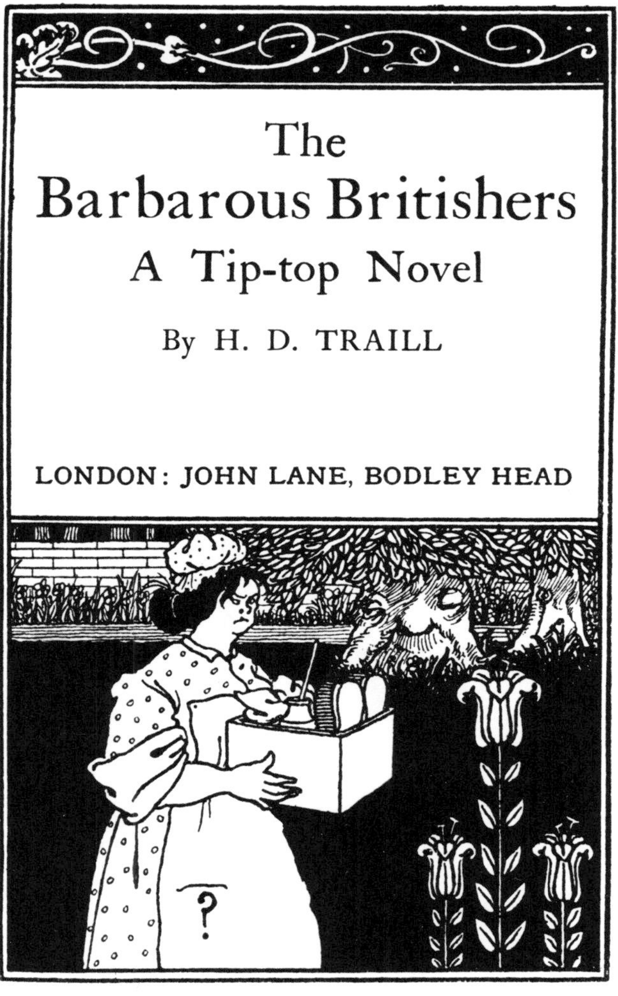

H[enry]. D[uff]. Traill, *The Barbarous Britishers. A Tip-top Novel*. London: John Lane, [1896]. Title-page. [checklist no. 98]

20 Miniature Posters.

DRAWN BY

AUBREY BEARDSLEY.

Representing the title designs of
the "Keynotes Series."

PRICE, $1.00 PER SET.

ROBERTS BROTHERS, Publishers, BOSTON.

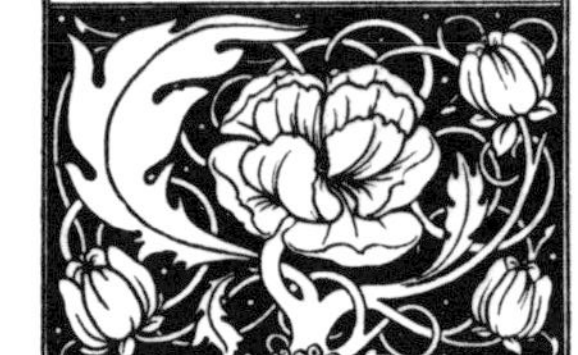

20 Miniature Posters. Drawn by Aubrey Beardsley. Representing the title designs of the "Keynotes Series." Boston: Roberts Brothers, [ca. 1896]. Front of envelope. [checklist no. 49]

49. 20 MINIATURE POSTERS. Drawn by Aubrey Beardsley. Representing the title designs of the "Keynotes Series." Price $1.00 per set. Boston: Roberts Brothers, [ca. 1896].[30]
By Beardsley: Reproductions in various colors of 20 of his 22 title-page designs for the Keynotes Series (American editions).
Loose sheets in cream envelope.   [G p. 43]
Notes: There was no English version. Described as "scarce" as early as 1923 when a copy was offered in the auction sale of John Quinn's library (Anderson Galleries, 12 November 1923, item 322).

50. "Becket." [1893].
Portrait of Henry Irving in the title role of Tennyson's eponymous play.
Etching and aquatint.   [R 52; R & D 146]
Notes: Not to be confused with a similar drawing reproduced in *The Pall Mall Budget*, checklist no. 9, this was the artist's sole original print.[31] A number of "proofs" were pulled from the copperplate [R & D 145], probably on more than one occasion. An example (at Harvard) is mounted in paper covers bearing the printed legend, "Thirty-five proofs only have now been taken from the original copper-plate in the possession of John Carter, each numbered and dated," and a manuscript note "No. 35. 1931."

51. Bookplate for John Lumsden Propert.[32] 1893.
Reproduced in Vol. 1 of *The Yellow Book*, April 1894. Legend reads "EX LIBRIS JOHN LVMSDEN PROPERT."
Line block.   [G 900; R 350; R & D 397; V 89 VIII; W 1]

52. **Björnstjerne Björnson**
PASTOR SANG. Being the Norwegian drama Over Aevne. Translated into English, for the author, by William Wilson. London: Longmans, Green, 1893.
By Beardsley: Frontispiece.
Tan cloth.   [G 845; R 264; R & D 289, 293; V 64]
Notes: Published in October 1893. "William Wilson" was the pseudonym of [William] More Adey (1858–1942), an acquaintance of Beardsley and close friend of Robert Ross and Oscar Wilde who published the first English version of Ibsen's *Brand* (1891) and who later became an art dealer and editor of *The Burlington Magazine*. The cover design is by Aymer Vallance.

---

[30] Title printed on front of envelope.
[31] *Letters* p. 58. Beardsley to Robert Ross, November [1893], "This morning Pennell has been giving me lessons in etching."
[32] Dr. John Lumsden Propert (1834–1902), physician, art critic, and collector of miniatures.

53. **Kenneth Grahame**
PAGAN PAPERS. London: Elkin Mathews and John Lane, 1894.
By Beardsley: Title-page design.
Green cloth.   [G 844; R 268; R & D 288, 292; V 67]
Notes: Published 30 November 1893 with postdated title-page. 615 copies.[33]
Author's first book.

54. THE PALL MALL BUDGET. No. 1319, 4 January 1894.
By Beardsley: "A New Year's Dream, After Studying Mr. Pennell's 'Devils of
Notre Dame'" in article, "The New Society of Illustrators."
Yellow wrappers.   [G 279; V 55 XIII]
Notes: Caricature of Joseph Pennell mimicking his 1893 etching, "Le Stryge."

55. MEDIÆVAL LEGENDS NO. II: THE WONDERFUL HIS-
TORY OF VIRGILIUS THE SORCERER OF ROME. En-
glished for the first time. London: David Nutt, 1893.
By Beardsley: Frontispiece.
Light brown wrappers.   [G 858; R 267; R & D 286, 294; V 63]
Notes: Published in January 1894.[34] Beardsley's frontispiece is said to have
been placed only in a large paper edition limited to 100 copies. However, the
publisher's advertisement[35] speaks, not of large and small paper issues, but of
a single edition, "16mo., 78 pp., red and black wrapper. 1s." of which "500
copies will be issued with a frontispiece by Aubrey Beardsley, price 3s. 6d."
for which "Immediate application should be made...." The anonymous
translation is by Mary Leighton.[36]

56. The Playgoers' Club. Tenth annual dinner, The Criterion, Jan. 28, 1894.
By Beardsley: Five drawings on outer pages [1] and [4] of folded menu card
for dinner held at The Criterion restaurant, London. The legend at the foot
of p. [4] reads "DESIGN BY AUBREY BEARDSLEY." (at left) and "PRO-
DUCED BY CARL HENTSCHEL." (at right).
Folded leaf.   [R 271; R & D 434]

---

[33] Nelson p. 287, no. 73 in his checklist. Some copies have a slip pasted to the front free endpaper
reading "Of this Edition 450 Copies have been printed for England."
[34] *Letters* p. 58. In a letter to Robert Ross dated by the editors "[late] November [1893]" Beardsley
writes, "I have just turned out a very amusing frontispiece to *Vergilius the Sorcerer* (Nutt)...."
[35] *The Bookman* (December 1893), p. 66.
[36] (1845–1946), woman of letters. See André Raffalovich, *Letters to Edward Playfair*, with a foreword and notes by Brocard Sewell and an introduction by Philip Healy (1982), note 3 on p. [38].

57. A CATALOGUE OF BOOKS PUBLISHED BY J. M. DENT
& CO. London: J. M. Dent, [1894].
By Beardsley: Front cover adapted from border for *Le Morte Darthur* (p. 155
of the first edition).
Cream wrappers.

58. **John Davidson**
PLAYS. Being: An unhistorical pastoral. A romantic farce. Bruce a chron-
icle play. Smith a tragic farce. And Scaramouch in Naxos a pantomime. Lon-
don: Elkin Mathews and John Lane, 1894.
By Beardsley: Frontispiece and title-page vignette (repeated on front cover).
Plum cloth.   [G 936–37; R 317–18; R & D 428, 430; V 88]
Notes: Published 12 February 1894. 760 copies.[37] A few copies were bound
in white cloth. Beardsley's frontispiece is believed to depict (from left to
right) Mabel Beardsley, Henry Harland (future literary editor of *The Yellow
Book*), Oscar Wilde, Sir Augustus Harris (theatrical manager), Richard Le
Gallienne, and the dancer Adeline Genée.[38] According to Reade and Dickinson, a small dot found on the back of Genée's skirt is "part of the line-
block" and may denote an early copy of the book. Criticism of the frontispiece led to a letter from Beardsley to *The Daily Chronicle*, checklist no. 61.

59. **Oscar Wilde**
SALOME. A tragedy in one act. Translated from the French of Oscar
Wilde. Pictured by Aubrey Beardsley. London: Elkin Mathews and John
Lane, 1894.
By Beardsley: 13 illustrations (including designs for frontispiece, title-page, list
of pictures, and tailpiece) and front and back (artist's three-candle device)
cover ornaments.   [G pp. 46–48; R 274–83; R & D 360–61; V 86]

ORDINARY ISSUE   [M 350; R & D 364]
Blue cloth. 755 copies (500 for England) printed on wove paper.

LARGE PAPER ISSUE   [M 351; R 273; R & D 365]
Green silk.[39] 125 copies (100 for England) printed on Japan vellum.

---

[37] An edition of 700 copies, 500 for England, the rest presumably for export (Nelson p. 288, no.
80 in his checklist).
[38] The identifications of Mabel Beardsley (initially made by R. A. Walker), Le Gallienne, and
Genée are all somewhat uncertain, and the faun figure, generally believed to represent Harland,
may in fact, as Brian Reade has argued, be a self-portrait of the artist. See Simon Wilson,
Beardsley, checklist no. 205A, note to Pl. 24.
[39] Reade Pl. 271 reproduces the front cover of a large paper copy.

Notes: Published 24 February 1894.[40] This was not only the first edition with Beardsley's drawings but also the first English edition, the first illustrated edition, and the first edition in English—*Salomé* having appeared in French a year earlier almost to the day. It is dedicated "To my friend Lord Alfred Bruce Douglas, the translator of my play," although his translation was so poor it had to be amended by Wilde and maybe others. Wilde is caricatured in "The Woman in the Moon" (frontispiece), "A Platonic Lament," "Enter Herodias," and "The Eyes of Herod." One of the intended drawings, "John and Salome," was replaced with "The Black Cape"—a design irrelevant to the play. The title-page and "Enter Herodias" were "bowdlerized" at the publisher's request, leading Beardsley to compose a bit of doggerel:

> Because one figure was undressed
> This little drawing was suppressed.
> It was unkind, but never mind,
> Perhaps it was for the best.[41]

59A. [ANOTHER EDITION]. San Francisco: The Paper Covered Book Store, 1896.
By Beardsley: 13 illustrations from first edition, checklist no. 59; title-page design appears on front cover and tailpiece is reproduced on back cover.
White wrappers. [G p. 48]
Notes: Published (in fact by Warren E. Price) 17 October 1896.

59B. [ANOTHER EDITION]. London: Melmoth & Co., 1904.
By Beardsley: 16 illustrations: the 13 from first edition, checklist no. 59, with the addition of the original cover design for *Salome,* "John and Salome," and "The Toilette of Salome II."

ORDINARY ISSUE [G p. 48; M 615]
Blue linen boards. 250 numbered copies.

LARGE PAPER ISSUE [G p. 48; M 616]
Blue cloth. 50 numbered copies printed on Japan vellum.

---

[40] Nelson p. 288, no. 81 in his checklist. Rupert Hart-Davis, in *The Letters of Oscar Wilde* (1962), note on p. 344 agrees with Mason and gives the date of publication as 9 February.

[41] Gallatin pp. 47–48, also R 285 and R & D 366, where the doggerel is quoted from the proof (in the Gallatin collection at Princeton) inscribed by Beardsley to Alfred Lambart. Frank Harris apparently received a similar proof inscribed with the same verse. Another presumably contemporary example of the "Enter Herodias" proof, printed on Japan vellum and bearing the printed initials of the engraver Carl Hentschel, was offered for sale and reproduced—with similar proofs of "John and Salome" and "The Toilette of Salome"—in Maggs Bros. cat. 1108, *Books of the Nineties* (1990), item 34. Smithers later produced a "forgery" of the "Enter Herodias" proof in an edition reputedly limited to 75 copies; this was printed on thinner paper, omits the engraver's initials, and "lacks the markings on the musical instrument."

Notes: Piracy in fact published by Smithers and sold by "Wright and Jones." Lane, who held the copyright, claimed he had a large portion of the edition seized and destroyed. Prospectus reproduces title-page and list of pictures.

59C. [ANOTHER EDITION]. London: John Lane, 1906.
By Beardsley: Front cover (and dust jacket) reproduces list of pictures design from first edition, checklist no. 59.
Grey boards, dust jacket.   [M 352]
Notes: Published in June 1906. Does not contain the illustrations.

59D. [ANOTHER EDITION]. With sixteen drawings by Aubrey Beardsley. London: John Lane, 1907.
By Beardsley: 16 illustrations from Smithers's "Melmoth & Co." edition, checklist no. 59B. Front cover reproduces original cover design for *Salome*.
Light green cloth.   [G p. 48; M 355]
Notes: Published in September 1906 with postdated title-page. Lane's second edition with Beardsley illustrations, the text of the play revised. Also contains a note on *Salome* by Robert Ross and programs for the first English production (10 May 1905) and for Richard Strauss's opera (9 December 1905). Reprinted by Lane in 1912 [M 356].

59E. A PORTFOLIO OF AUBREY BEARDSLEY'S DRAW-INGS ILLUSTRATING "SALOME" BY OSCAR WILDE. [London: John Lane, 1906].
By Beardsley: 17 illustrations: the 16 from Lane's 1907 edition, checklist no. 59D, with a hitherto unpublished additional drawing, "Salome on Settle."
Loose plates printed on Japan vellum in parchment-backed grey cloth portfolio. [G p. 48; R 272, 284, 286, 288–90; R & D 344–59, 363, 448; V 86 XIII]
Notes: Published in September? 1906. Front cover ornament from first edition stamped on front cover. "Some time after the publication of this portfolio a list of the seventeen plates [incorporating the title] was printed and issued with the remaining sets,"[42] presumably forming a second "issue."

59F. [ANOTHER EDITION]. New York: F. M. Buckles & Co., 1906.
By Beardsley: Front cover reproduces title-page design from first edition, checklist no. 59.
Cream wrappers.
Notes: Does not contain the illustrations.

---

[42] Mason p. 384. In *Catalogue 165: Books from the Library of John Lane and other Books of the Eigh-teen-Nineties*, checklist no. 180, item 55 is described as "Illustrations to Salome. Printed on Jap-anese vellum…in original half-parchment portfolio, as issued [Sept. 14, 1906]. One of a few copies published before the plates were numbered, and without any index, list of plates, etc."

59G. SALOME. A tragedy in one act. Drawings by Aubrey Beardsley. Boston: John W. Luce, 1906.
Black cloth.   [G p. 48]
By Beardsley: 13 illustrations from first edition, checklist no. 59.
Notes: Published 3 November 1906. Front cover reproduces detail from "John and Salome."

59H. [ANOTHER EDITION]. Boston: John W. Luce, 1907.
By Beardsley: 16 illustrations from Lane's 1907 edition, checklist no. 59D.
Black cloth.
Notes: Front cover reproduces detail from "John and Salome." Facsimiles of this edition were published by Bruce Humphries, Boston, in 1964? and by Branden Publishing Company, Boston, in 1989.

59I. SALOME. Drame en un acte. Édition à petit nombre. Paris: Imprimée pour les souscripteurs, 1907.
By Beardsley: 16 illustrations from Lane's 1907 edition, checklist no. 59D.

ORDINARY ISSUE   [G p. 48; M 618]
Green wrappers, printed label on front cover. Nos. 101–500 of 500 numbered copies printed on Arches paper.

SPECIAL ISSUE   [G p. 48; M 618]
Green wrappers. Nos. 1–100 of 500 numbered copies printed on antique English paper.

Notes: Despite a slip stating that Robert Ross and Methuen approved of its issue, this is an unauthorized edition, issued by Charles Carrington, Paris.[43]

59J. [ANOTHER EDITION]. Tragodie in einem akte von Oscar Wilde. Ins Deutsche ubertragen von Hedwig Lachmann. Mit funfzehn zeichnungen von Aubrey Beardsley. Leipzig: Insel-Verlag, [1907].

ORDINARY ISSUE
725 numbered copies.

SPECIAL ISSUE
Reversed calf. 100 numbered copies printed on Japan vellum.

Notes: Reprinted by Insel-Verlag in 1919, 1924, and 1959.

59K. [ANOTHER EDITION]. With sixteen drawings by Aubrey Beardsley. London: John Lane, 1912.
By Beardsley: 16 illustrations from Lane's 1907 edition, checklist no. 59D.
Green cloth, grey dust jacket.   [M 527]

---

[43] Mason 619 transcribes title-page of another unauthorized reprint published by Carrington.

Notes: Published 10 November 1911 with postdated title-page. Lane's third edition with illustrations, forming part of Methuen's 1909 second collected edition of Wilde's works.[44]

59L. [ANOTHER EDITION]. Pictured by Aubrey Beardsley. Boston: John W. Luce, 1912.
By Beardsley: 15 illustrations (lacking the cover design) from Lane's 1907 edition, checklist no. 59D.
Lavender cloth.   [M 458]
Notes: Text from Luce's unillustrated version, published in one volume with *A Florentine Tragedy* and *Vera* in 1910. This was an authorized edition, based on the collected works issued by Methuen in 1908. Warrack and Perkins 38 gives different information. Front cover reproduces "John and Salome."

59M. [ANOTHER EDITION]. Tragedya w jednym akcie. Slowo wstepne i przeklad Leona Choromanskiego. Illustracye Aubrey Beardsley'a. Warsaw: F. Hoesick, 1914.   [G p. 48]
Notes: Polish translation.

59N. [ANOTHER EDITION]. Tragodie in 1 akt. Mit 16 zeichnungen von Aubrey Beardsley. Deutsch von Paul Steegemann. Hannover: Heinrich Böhme, 1918.
By Beardsley: 16 illustrations from Lane's 1907 edition, checklist no. 59D.

ORDINARY ISSUE
Dark blue (also brown) calf. Nos. 251–1,000 of 1,000 numbered copies.

SPECIAL ISSUES
Vellum, sewn over thongs; top edges gilt. Copies nos. 1–100 printed on Flemish paper, nos. 101–250 printed on antique paper.

59O. [ANOTHER EDITION]. Tragodie in 1 akt. Mit 16 zeichnungen von Aubrey Beardsley. Deutsch von Curt Moreck. Hannover: Heinrich Böhme, 1919.
Notes: This may in fact be the same as the preceding entry, checklist no. 59N.

59P. [ANOTHER EDITION]. With sixteen drawings by Aubrey Beardsley. London: John Lane, 1920.
By Beardsley: 16 illustrations from Lane's 1907 edition, checklist no. 59D.
Front cover reproduces original cover design for *Salome*.
Red cloth, pale green dust jacket.   [G p. 48]

---

[44] The front cover (and dust jacket) bears an ornamental design by Charles Ricketts, first used on the limited edition of *De Profundis* (1905); see M p. 507.

Notes: Lane's fourth edition with illustrations, produced in large format to match his edition of *Under the Hill and Other Essays in Prose and Verse,* checklist no. 141. Contains Robert Ross's note on *Salome* and programs for the first English production and for Richard Strauss's opera, first published in Lane's 1907 edition, checklist no. 59D. Reprinted by Lane in 1927 and 1930.

59Q. SALOME. Tragedie en un acte par Oscar Wilde. Illustrations d'Aubrey Beardsley. Boston: John W. Luce, 1920.
By Beardsley: 16 illustrations from Lane's 1907 edition, checklist no. 59D.
Red cloth.
Notes: The illustrations are unexpurgated and possibly doctored. Front cover reproduces detail from "John and Salome."

59R. SALOME AND OTHER STORIES. Illustrations by Aubrey Beardsley. London: Gold Medal Library, [after 1920?].
By Beardsley: Frontispiece and eight illustrations.
Brown cloth.   [G pp. 48–49]

59S. SALOME. Drame en un acte. Paris: Edition à petit nombre réservée aux souscripteurs et non mise dans le commerce [Alençon, Corbière, & Jugain], 1920.
By Beardsley: 16 illustrations from Lane's 1920 edition, checklist no. 59P (including facsimiles of the title-page and list of pictures with letterpress).
Purple wrappers, printed label on front cover.

ORDINARY ISSUE
250 numbered copies printed on Arches paper.

SPECIAL ISSUE
35 numbered copies printed on Japan vellum (also five not for sale). Plates in two states.

59T. [ANOTHER EDITION]. Book Collector's Association, [1927?].

59U. [ANOTHER EDITION]. [Tokyo: English Student Newspaper, 1929].
Notes: Text in English and Japanese (translation by Arakawa Kinnosuko).

59V. [ANOTHER EDITION]. New York: Williams, Belasco, and Meyers, 1930.
By Beardsley: 16 illustrations from Lane's 1907 edition, checklist no. 59D.
Blue cloth.   [G p. 48]

59W. [ANOTHER EDITION]. New York: Halcyon House, [1930?].

59X. [ANOTHER EDITION]. New York: Illustrated Editions Company, [1931].
By Beardsley: 16 (expurgated) illustrations from Lane's 1907 edition, checklist no. 59D.
Black cloth-backed red cloth, dust jacket. [G pp. 48–49]
Notes: Dust jacket reproduces "The Peacock Skirt." The same typesetting and printer (J. J. Little & Ives, New York) were used for a version published by the Three Sirens Press, New York, also 1931? (bound in purple cloth-backed blue boards, also blue suede-backed yellow cloth), of which there was an issue or impression limited to 1,500 numbered copies.

59Y. [ANOTHER EDITION]. Cleveland: World Publishing Company, [1931?].
Notes: Reprinted by Gaslight Press, Grand Rapids, Mich., in 1969.

59Z. INKYOKU SAROME. Tokyo: Randai Sambo, 1938.
Notes: Japanese translation (by Konosuke Hinatsu, possibly a pseudonym). Fourth edition was published by Kadokawa Shoten, Tokyo, in 1954.

59AA. SALOME. A tragedy in one act. Translated from the French of Oscar Wilde by Lord Alfred Douglas and illustrated by Aubrey Beardsley. With a new introduction by Holbrook Jackson. London: Printed for the members of the Limited Editions Club, 1938.
By Beardsley: 16 illustrations from Lane's 1907 portfolio, checklist no. 59E.
Red boards in slipcase. [G p. 49]
Notes: 1,500 numbered copies printed by Fanfare Press, London. Front cover design incorporates original cover for *Salome.* Issued with companion volume containing French *Salomé* illustrated by André Derain (1,500 numbered copies signed by Derain, black wrappers, printed by Dehon et Cie, Paris).

59AB. [ANOTHER EDITION]. Tragedi i 1 akt, med 16 teckningar av Aubrey Beardsley. Stockholm: Bibliofila Klubben, 1946.

ORDINARY ISSUE
500 numbered copies.

SPECIAL ISSUE
50 numbered copies.

Notes: Swedish translation.

59AC. [ANOTHER EDITION]. New York: Hartsdale House, [1947?].

59AD. [ANOTHER EDITION]. Drame en un acte par Oscar Wilde. Avec quinze dessins par Aubrey Beardsley. Socking [?]: Heinrich F. S. Bachmair, 1949.
Notes: 2,100 copies.

59AE. [ANOTHER EDITION]. Garden City, N. Y.: Halcyon House, [1950?].

59AF. [ANOTHER EDITION]. Translated and introduced by R. A. Walker. Illustrations by Aubrey Beardsley. [London:] Heinemann, [1957].
By Beardsley: 18 illustrations: the 17 from Lane's 1907 portfolio, checklist no. 59E (substituting the unexpurgated version of "Enter Herodias") and "J'ai Baisé Ta Bouche Jokanaan: Salomé with the Head of John the Baptist," from *The Studio*, April 1893, checklist no. 16.
Black cloth, dust jacket.
Notes: Published 9 December 1957. Contains *all* the illustrations in their original form. Front and back covers reproduce cover ornaments from first edition, checklist no. 59; jacket front reproduces design from contents page.

59AG. SAROME. Tokyo: Shincho Sha, 1958.
Notes: Japanese translation (by Tsuneari Fukuda). Another edition? published by Iwanami Shoten, Tokyo, in 1959

59AH. SALOME. Drame en un acte. Paris: Éditions du Colombier, [1966].
By Beardsley: 16 illustrations from Lane's 1907 portfolio, checklist no. 59E.
Cream cloth.
Notes: 1,500 numbered copies. Front cover reproduces "The Black Cape."

59AI. [ANOTHER EDITION]. New York: Dover, [1967].
By Beardsley: 20 illustrations: the 17 from Lane's 1907 portfolio, checklist no. 59E, plus the front and back cover ornaments from first edition, checklist no. 59, and "J'ai Baisé Ta Bouche Jokanaan: Salomé with the Head of John the Baptist," from *The Studio*, April 1893, checklist no. 16.
Cream wrappers printed in orange.
Notes: Described as a facsimile of the 1894 first edition, this volume is in fact an amalgam of text and illustrations from various editions, also incorporating Robert Ross's note on *Salome* from Lane's 1920 edition, checklist no. 59P.

59AJ. [ANOTHER EDITION]. Barcelona: Editorial Lumen, 1979.
Notes: Spanish translation.

59AK. SALOMEH. Tragedyah be-maarakhah ahat tirgemah min ha-makor ha-Tsorfati Bosmat Alon; iyurim mekoriyim me-et Ovri Birdsli. Jerusalem: Bet hotsaah Elisar, 1981.

59AL. SALOME. Translated from the French by Lord Alfred Douglas. With an introduction by Steven Berkoff. Illustrations by Aubrey Beardsley. London: Faber and Faber, [1989].
By Beardsley: 13 illustrations, including original cover design for *Salome.*
White wrappers.
Notes: In part a facsimile of Lane's 1907 edition, checklist no. 59D, with Robert Ross's note. Front cover reproduces "The Climax."

60. ST. PAUL'S. Vol. 1, No. 1, March 1894.
By Beardsley: Three drawings (done in 1893): "Music" (headpiece), "Design for a Headpiece," and "The Man that Holds the Watering Pot" (tailpiece).
Wrappers.   [G 280–81, 283; R 291–93; R & D 287, 290–91; V 71]
Notes: "Music" and "The Man that Holds the Watering Pot" were reprinted in the 2 April 1898 issue of the magazine. "Design for a Headpiece," as it appears here, as well as in the 9 April 1898 issue of *St. Paul's* and in *The Early Work,* checklist no. 133, omits the fetus and glass jar found in the original drawing.

61. THE DAILY CHRONICLE. 2 March 1894.
By Beardsley: Letter to the editor, dated 1 March 1894, a reply to criticism of his frontispiece for John Davidson's *Plays,* checklist no. 58. Reprinted in *Letters.*

62. Poster to advertise the joint production of *A Comedy of Sighs* by John Todhunter and *The Land of Heart's Desire* by W. B. Yeats, Avenue Theatre, London, 29 March 1894.
By Beardsley: Drawing of a woman standing behind a curtain. Handlettered name of the theater almost certainly by Beardsley.
Color lithograph.   [G 788; R 319; R & D 383; V 76]
Notes: Gives titles, opening date, and cast lists of the two plays. The name of the printer, Stafford & Co., Nottingham, is found in the bottom right corner of the poster. Early in 1894 the actress (and novelist) Florence Farr "commissioned Beardsley to design the programme for *A Comedy of Sighs*[45] by John Todhunter which was produced at the Avenue Theatre on 29 March 1894 with W. B. Yeats's *The Land of Heart's Desire* as curtain-raiser." The drawing Beardsley made was used for this poster—here termed the "Avenue Theatre poster" for convenience—promoting the Todhunter–Yeats double bill,[46] again for the poster and program for the inaugural run of George Bernard

---

[45] On the poster the play's title is given as "A Comedy of Sighs!"
[46] In 1966 Anthony d'Offay issued a facsimile of this poster; see notes on the poster to advertise the Keynotes Series, checklist no. 47, and footnote 29, page 26.

Shaw's *Arms and the Man,* and also for the first edition of *The Land of Heart's Desire.*[47] Vallance notes that the Avenue Theatre poster "has since [between 1894 and 1909] been printed, original size, in black and white."[48] The parodist (and later editor of *Punch*) Owen Seaman made fun of Beardsley's design in his "Ars Postera," which begins:

> Mr. Aubrey Beer de Beers,
>   You're getting quite a high renown;
> Your Comedy of Leers, you know,
>   Is posted all about the town;
> This kind of stuff I cannot puff,
>   As Boston says, it makes me "tired";
> Your Japanee-Rossetti girl
>   Is not a thing to be desired.[49]

62A. Program for *A Comedy of Sighs* by John Todhunter and *The Land of Heart's Desire* by W. B. Yeats, Avenue Theatre, London, 29 March 1894.
By Beardsley: Design for the Avenue Theatre poster, checklist no. 62, reproduced (in blue) on first page.
Folded leaf of pale green paper.   [G 788; R & D 368; V 76]
Notes: Legend printed at lower left below design reads "Designed by AUBREY BEARDSLEY." Reade and Dickinson state that the artist's name is "spelt BEARDSLEYS" —an error corrected in the versions of the program used to advertise *Arms and the Man,* checklists nos. 62C and 62D. With the imprint of the printer, David Allen and Sons, London, on last page.

62B. Poster to advertise the joint production of *Arms and the Man* by George Bernard Shaw and *The Land of Heart's Desire* by W. B. Yeats, Avenue Theatre, London, 21 April 1894.
By Beardsley: Reuses design for the Avenue Theatre poster, checklist no. 62. Black and white lithograph.
Notes: In 1929 the London bookseller W. & G. Foyle offered for sale in their *A Catalogue of Old & Rare Books* (1929) a quantity of "proofs" for this

[47] *Letters* p. 63, note 2. From Beardsley's letter to Farr, dated to February 1894, it seems likely that he was originally asked to provide a drawing for the program, not the poster: "I think you will find dark green on light the most satisfactory scheme of colour. Of course I should make my design in black and white, so that a zinc block can be made, and from that you can print in any colour you like. By the way, if my design is going to be used as a poster had I not better draw it large size and have it reduced for programme?" The poster is placed first here because it was undoubtedly circulated before the performance, at which the program would have been distributed.
[48] Vallance 76. The design was later reproduced in *The Idler,* March 1897, checklist no. 114.
[49] First published anonymously in *Punch* (21 April 1894), with a drawing burlesquing the poster, reprinted in Seaman's *The Battle of the Bays* (1896).

poster—described as having been purchased directly from George Bernard Shaw, then the owner of the original drawing. These lacked the letterpress titles and cast lists of the plays and were clearly posthumous (and possibly fraudulent) in nature, bearing only the words "DESIGNED BY THE LATE AUBREY BEARDSLEY" and the printer's name.

62C. Program for *Arms and the Man* by George Bernard Shaw and *The Land of Heart's Desire* by W. B. Yeats, Avenue Theatre, London, 21 April 1894.
By Beardsley: Design for the Avenue Theatre poster, checklist no. 62, reproduced (in dark blue) on first page.
Folded leaf of pale green paper.   [G 788; R & D 369; V 76]
Notes: Legend printed at lower left below design reads "Designed by AUBREY BEARDSLEY." With the imprint of the printer, David Allen and Sons, London, on last page.

62D. Program for *Arms and the Man* by George Bernard Shaw and *The Man in the Street* by Louis N. Parker, Avenue Theatre, London, [May 1894].
By Beardsley: Design for the Avenue Theatre poster, checklist no. 62, reproduced (in black) on first page.
Folded leaf of cream paper.
Notes: Front cover design and text printed within red rule border. Same legend and imprint as previous programs, checklist nos. 62A and 62C.[50]

62E. **W[illiam]. B[utler]. Yeats**[51]
THE LAND OF HEART'S DESIRE. London: T. Fisher Unwin, 1894.
By Beardsley: Design for the Avenue Theatre poster, checklist no. 62, reproduced (without lettering) on front cover and title-page.
Mauve wrappers.   [V 76]
Notes: Published in April 1894 (May, according to *The English Catalogue*).[52] 500 copies. There are two binding variants, one (believed by some to be the earliest) with no fleurons after the word "DESIRE" on front cover, the other (much less common) with two fleurons; some copies have a slip inserted giv-

---

[50] *The Man in the Street* replaced Yeats's play on 14 May and continued as curtain-raiser to the end of the run of *Arms and the Man* on 7 July 1894.

[51] In 1896 Beardsley began a series of six illustrations for Yeats's play, *The Shadowy Waters*, then planned for publication by Leonard Smithers. He only completed one drawing. See *Letters* pp. 186 and 215, note 3.

[52] On 15 April 1894 Yeats wrote to John O'Leary, "My little play 'The Land of Hearts Desire' is considered a fair success & is to be put on again with the play by Shaw which goes on next week. It is being printed by Unwin & will be sold at the Theatre with the programes" (W. B. Yeats, *The Collected Letters of W. B. Yeats: Volume One, 1865–1895*, ed. John Kelly [1986], p. 386). Publication therefore probably took place on or around 21 April, when *Arms and the Man* opened.

ing the net price and stating that the book was not be sold at a discount.[53]
Beardsley's design was used as the frontispiece in the first American edition
(450 copies, bound in grey boards, printed label on spine) published by Stone
and Kimball, Chicago, in late summer or early fall 1894.[54]

63. ST. PAUL'S. 2 April 1894.
By Beardsley: "Girl at Her Toilet." Reprinted as "La Dame aux Camélias" in
Vol. III of *The Yellow Book,* October 1894. Later colored by the artist and re-
produced in this form in *A Book of Fifty Drawings,* checklist no. 112.[55]
Wrappers.   [G 916; R 322; V 89 XXI]

64. THE SKETCH. Vol. V, No. 63, 11 April 1894.
By Beardsley: Three drawings, in interview with Beardsley and Henry Har-
land entitled "What the 'Yellow Book' Is To Be: Some Meditations with Its
Editors": front cover design for Vol. I of *The Yellow Book,* "Mr. Aubrey
Beardsley" (self-portrait), and "Mr. Henry Harland."
Cream wrappers.   [G 930-31; V 80-81]

65. THE YELLOW BOOK. An illustrated quarterly. Vols. I and II: Lon-
don: Elkin Mathews and John Lane, April and July 1894. Vols. III and IV:
London: John Lane, October 1894 and January 1895.
Yellow cloth.   [G pp. 49-53]

VOL. I, April 1894. [G 893-900; R 343-50; R & D 411, 416; V 89 II-VIII]
By Beardsley: Four drawings, front cover, back cover, spine,[56] and title-page
designs.

[53] Allan Wade, *A Bibliography of the Writings of W. B. Yeats,* third edition, revised and edited by
Russell K. Alspach (1968), item 10, pp. 30-32. The information on the number of copies printed comes from A. J. A. Symons, who mentioned what may be an additional "60 in loose wrappers" of which Wade could not locate an example.
[54] Wade item 11, p. 32. The title-page is misdated "MDCCCXIV" in place of "MDCCCXCIV." Sidney Kramer, *A History of Stone & Kimball and Herbert S. Stone & Co.: With a Bibliography of Their
Publications, 1893-1905* (1940), item 25, p. 215, notes that this was the first title issued after the
publisher's move to Chicago and the first to incorporate the specially watermarked paper with
initials "s" and "k." See also Charles Gullans and John Espey, "Some New Problems in the Study
of Herbert S. Stone & Co., with Further Additions to Kramer's *Stone & Kimball,*" *PBSA* (1991),
p. 153, who "conclude that electrotype plates were made by Unwin and sent to the University
Press, Cambridge, where the Stone & Kimball edition was printed."
[55] The drawing, to which Beardsley added watercolor washes sometime in the period 1894-97,
is generally known by its second title.
[56] Vols. I-V all share the same back cover design [R 344], the publishers' initials "EM" and "JL"
removed after Vol. II. The design for the spine of Vol. I is repeated on Vol. II, while that for Vol.
III is repeated on Vols. IV and V.

Notes: Published 16 April 1894. Criticism of the title-page design and of one of the illustrations, a portrait of Mrs. Patrick Campbell, led to letters from Beardsley to the editors of *The Pall Mall Budget,* checklist no. 68, and *The Daily Chronicle,* checklist no. 66, respectively.

VOL. II, July 1894.   [G 901–8; R 351–59; R & D 412, 417; V 89 IX–XIV]
By Beardsley: Six drawings, front cover, back cover, spine, and title-page designs.

VOL. III, October 1894.   [G 909–17; R 322, 360–64; R & D 413, 420;
V 89 XV–XXII]
By Beardsley: Six drawings (including the artist's "Portrait of Himself"), front cover, back cover, spine, and title-page designs.
Notes: Two drawings are signed using the names of imaginary artists: "Mantegna" as by Philip Broughton and "From a Pastel" as by Albert Foschter.

VOL. IV, January 1895.   [G 918–23; R 365–70; R & D 414, 424;
V 89 XXIII–XXVIII]
By Beardsley: Four drawings, front cover, back cover, spine, and title-page designs.
Notes: Published ca. 16 January 1895.

VOL. V, April 1895.   [G pp. 52–53; R 371; R & D 415]
By Beardsley: Back cover and spine designs (repeated from Vol. IV), left on by mistake after the artist's dismissal (see notes below).

Notes: Beardsley served as art editor for the first four of 13 volumes of this most famous British magazine of the 1890s (of which Henry Harland was literary editor), until his dismissal in April 1895 in the wake of Oscar Wilde's arrest.[57] His position was taken over personally by the publisher, John Lane, who relied on another prolific graphic artist employed by the Bodley Head, Patten Wilson (1868–1928), for expertise and advice. (Wilson's work—especially for the Keynotes Series—is sometimes mistaken for Beardsley's own.) Volume V of *The Yellow Book,*[58] due out in mid-April 1895, was in production when Beardsley was fired. His contributions were removed (except for the back cover and spine designs, first used for Vol. III, which were inadvertently left in place) and replaced with work by other artists.

[57] See R & D 426, 484–85; Margaret D. Stetz and Mark Samuels Lasner, *The Yellow Book: A Centenary Exhibition* (1994), pp. 30–32; and Ella D'Arcy, *Some Letters to John Lane,* ed. Alan Anderson (1990), pp. 15–19.
[58] A sole surviving "dummy" copy of Vol. V of *The Yellow Book,* inscribed by Harland and by a former owner, Edmund Gosse, and containing Beardsley's illustrations, title-page, and cover design, is in the Gallatin collection at Princeton (G pp. 52–53; R & D 426). For the original drawing intended for the front cover and prospectus, see R & D 404.

As the publisher admitted in 1949, reprints of *The Yellow Book* had long been "circulated in what can only be described as irregular methods and passed off as first editions."[59] These later impressions and facsimiles are difficult to identify. Differences in the thickness of the volumes, the position of contents leaves, the typesetting, the placement of signature markings, the illustrations, the binding, and the paper have all been noted,[60] but so many sets have been "made up" and the details are so perplexing that rational codification may well prove impossible. It appears, however, that since the "original" volumes—those actually printed during the magazine's run—contained publishers' advertisements bound in at the back, no volume *without* the ads can be a first edition. Copies of the first few volumes sometimes appear with a later edition appellation ("Second Edition," etc.) stamped on the front cover.[61] These assuredly are "originals" (plausibly demarcating subsequent legitimate impressions of the first edition), as are copies of Vol. i with the misprint "Aprtl" for "April" on the front cover.

65A. Prospectus for *The Yellow Book,* Vol. i, April 1894.
By Beardsley: Front cover design.
Yellow wrappers.   [G 926; R 342; R & D 410; V 89 1]
Notes: Two variants, possibly denoting "states," have been recorded. One, in light yellow wrappers, asserts in the last paragraph of the text that the subscription price will be "postage paid"; the other, in dark yellow wrappers, omits the words "postage paid." Another version, described by one source as "issued privately," has light yellow wrappers and the cover design printed on a larger panel [R & D 409].

According to Reade, "The suggestion contained in the design is that the enterprising young woman who is free to decide what she reads will be interested in just this sort of periodical.... The elderly pierrot looking on from the doorway was said to represent Elkin Mathews, partner of John Lane at the Bodley Head."[62]

---

[59] "Bibliographic Note" in *The Yellow Book: A Selection,* comp. Norman Denny (1949), p. [13]. According to the *Bibliography of American Literature,* one of the later reprints was made by the bookseller Charles J. Sawyer, in 1927. Another London firm, Henry Sotheran, circulated an elaborate brochure offering sets and may also have produced an unacknowledged facsimile.

[60] For example, the front cover is stamped in *dark green* (not black) on copies of Vol. ii from the "original" issue.

[61] Nelson pp. 322–23 provides a transcript of the final inventory made at the breakup of the Mathews and Lane partnership. According to this document, as of 30 June 1894 the total number of copies printed of Vol. i (published 16 April 1894) was 7,000 and of Vol. ii 5,000. These figures come early in the history of the magazine and do not, of course, take into account any subsequent impressions and reprintings made by Lane once he had *The Yellow Book* under his sole control.

[62] Reade 342.

65B. Prospectus for *The Yellow Book,* Vol. II, July 1894.
By Beardsley: Front cover design (same as found on magazine).
Yellow wrappers.   [G p. 52]

65C. Prospectus for *The Yellow Book,* Vol. III, October 1894.
By Beardsley: Front cover design (same as found on magazine).
Yellow wrappers.   [G p. 52]

65D. Prospectus for *The Yellow Book,* Vol. IV, January 1895.
By Beardsley: Front cover design (same as found on magazine).
Yellow wrappers.   [G p. 52]

65E. Prospectus for *The Yellow Book,* Vol. V, April 1895.
By Beardsley: Front cover design, intended for Vol. V but not used.
Yellow wrappers.   [G 925 and p. 52; R 371; R & D 425]

65F. Poster to advertise *The Yellow Book,* Vol. I, April 1894.[63]
By Beardsley: Drawing of a standing woman holding a hat.
Line block on yellow paper.   [G 924; R 341; R & D 408; V 89 xxx]
Notes: Gives magazine's title, contents, and publisher, etc. Above the frame
are the words "SOLD HERE" and below "FIVE SHILLINGS NET." The engraver's name "C[ARL]. HENTSCHEL Sc" is found at the bottom left corner
of the design. Similar posters were made for later volumes, even after Beardsley's dismissal. Some examples issued by the magazine's American publishers, Copeland and Day of Boston, have a different arrangement, adding at
lower center the front cover design (in reduced size) of the volume being advertised and altering the letterpress. Facsimiles of both the Lane and Copeland and Day versions were published in 1966 by Anthony d'Offay.[64]

66. THE DAILY CHRONICLE. 17 April 1894.
By Beardsley: Letter to the editor, dated 16 April [1894], regarding his portrait of Mrs. Patrick Campbell (in Arthur Wing Pinero's play, *The Second
Mrs. Tanqueray*) published in Vol. I of *The Yellow Book,* April 1894. Reprinted
in Gallatin and in *Letters.*

67. TO-DAY. 28 April 1894.
By Beardsley: "Masked Pierrot and Female Figure," headpiece to "Stageland"
section. Used in a number of later issues. Reprinted in *Some Unknown Drawings of Aubrey Beardsley,* checklist no. 170.
Wrappers.   [G 934]

[63] See R & D 406 for the original drawing for another, unused poster design.
[64] For more information on d'Offay's reproductions, see footnote 29, page 26.

68. THE PALL MALL BUDGET. No. 1336, 3 May 1894.
By Beardsley: Letter to the editor, dated 27 April [1894], defending his title-page design for Vol. 1 of *The Yellow Book,* April 1894. Reprinted in *Letters.*
Yellow wrappers.

69. TO-DAY. 12 May 1894.
By Beardsley: "The Fat Woman," in interview with Beardsley, "A New Master of Art: Mr. Aubrey Beardsley." Also reprints "Masked Pierrot and Female Figure" headpiece to "Stageland" section.
Wrappers. [G 933–34; R 325; R & D 501, 504; V 83, 85]
Notes: "The Fat Woman," a caricature of James McNeill Whistler's wife Beatrix, was originally intended for Vol. 1 of *The Yellow Book,* April 1894.[65] The interview includes an unsigned drawing of Beardsley.

70. THE CAMBRIDGE A.B.C. Nos. 1–4. Cambridge: Elijah Johnson, June 1894.
By Beardsley: Front cover design, used on all four numbers.[66]
Cream wrappers.[67] [G 866; R 326; R & D 367; V 105]
Notes: Produced by Maurice Baring (the "B" of the title), with two other Cambridge students, Richard Austen Leigh ("A") and H. Warre Cornish ("C"). Beardsley received ten guineas for the drawing.[68] The issues are sometimes found bound up in green cloth with the design on the front cover.[69]

71. THE NEW REVIEW. Vol. XI, July 1894.
By Beardsley: Part III of "The Art of the Hoarding," an essay on posters (other parts by Jules Chérêt and Dudley Hardy), illustrated with two works: poster to advertise *The Yellow Book,* checklist no. 65F, and design later used for poster to advertise *The Spinster's Scrip,* checklist no. 92. Text reprinted in Gallatin and in R. A. Walker, *A Beardsley Miscellany,* checklist no. 190.
Wrappers.

72. **Jocelyn Quilp**
BARON VERDIGRIS. A romance of the reversed direction. With a frontispiece by Aubrey Beardsley. London: Henry, 1894.
By Beardsley: Frontispiece.
Green cloth. [G 787; R 328; R & D 427, 429; V 75]

---

[65] *Letters* pp. 65–66.
[66] The four issues are dated 8, 9, 11, and 12 June 1894.
[67] Copies may also exist bound in grey-green wrappers with the Beardsley design on front cover.
[68] *Letters* p. 67.
[69] As described in Norman Colbeck, *A Bookman's Catalogue: The Norman Colbeck Collection of Nineteenth Century and Edwardian Poetry and Belles Lettres* (1987), Vol. 1, p. 41.

Notes: Published in July 1894. The author's name is probably a pseudonym. Reprinted in Lane's Random Series in October 1897.

73. Invitation card for opening of the Prince's Ladies Golf Club. [Mitcham, Surrey, 16 July 1894].
    By Beardsley: Drawing (at left) of two women golfers with a pierrot as caddie. Letterpress (at right) reads "The Committee have the pleasure to invite [*blank line for name to be filled in*] and friend to the Opening of The Prince's Ladies Golf Club On [*blank line for date to be filled in*] 1894."[70]
    Line block on card. [G 874; R 329; R & D 502–3; V 106]

74. THE IDLER. "Advanced Woman Number," Vol. VI, September 1894.
    By Beardsley: Headpiece for "The Idler's Club" (repeated in smaller size on front cover) introducing a series of articles entitled "How to Court the 'Advanced Woman,'" beginning with "The Development of the 'Emancipated'" by Angus Evan Abbott.
    Wrappers. [G 943; R 330; R & D 436–37; V 97]

75. Poster to advertise T. Fisher Unwin's Children's Books. [1894].
    By Beardsley: Drawing of woman in armchair reading a book.
    Color lithograph. [G 781; R 335; R & D 297; V 78]
    Notes: Printed in black and light purple. Lists children's books and a periodical published or sold by T. Fisher Unwin. In its most common form it was used to advertise *Topsys and Turvys* by P. S. Newell, four works by Palmer Cox, the first 19 volumes in Unwin's Children's Library, *The Land of Pluck* by Mary Mapes Dodge, and the magazine *St. Nicholas.* According to Gallatin the poster was also produced in reduced size. A facsimile of the full-size version and a facsimile of the design without letterpress were among the group of Beardsley posters published in 1966 by Anthony d'Offay.[71]

    Copeland and Day also utilized Beardsley's drawing (printed in black and yellow) on a poster promoting *The Yellow Book*—not to be confused with checklist no. 65F. They did so without Unwin's authorization, a step which led to an acrimonious correspondence between the two publishers and threats of legal action after the design was reproduced in an article about posters published in the March 1896 issue of *The Overland Monthly,* an American periodical.

---

[70] Reproduced in J. Stephan Lawrence, Rare Books, *Catalogue Number 44: Aubrey Beardsley,* checklist no. 206, item 91, and in Sotheby's catalogue of *Illustrated and Children's Books, Juvenilia, and Related Drawings* (17–19 June 1987), p. 53.
[71] See footnote 29, page 26.

75A. GOOD READING ABOUT MANY BOOKS MOSTLY
BY THEIR AUTHORS. London: T. Fisher Unwin, 1894–95.
By Beardsley: Design for the poster to advertise T. Fisher Unwin's Children's
Books, checklist no. 75,[72] and the previously unpublished "Girl and a Book-
shop" (1893), drawing adapted and colored for poster to advertise Unwin's
Pseudonym and Autonym Libraries, checklist no. 76.
[G 790; R 334; R & D 380; V 77]

ORDINARY ISSUE
Light green cloth (also in wrappers).

LARGE PAPER ISSUE
Imitation vellum paper-backed blue-grey boards. 100 copies printed on Japan paper numbered and signed by T. Fisher Unwin.

Notes: Published in April 1895.

75B. **Anna Katharine Green [Rohlfs]**
THE DOCTOR, HIS WIFE, AND THE CLOCK. London: T.
Fisher Unwin, 1895.
By Beardsley: Front cover design (repeated on preliminary leaf) adapted from
poster to advertise T. Fisher Unwin's Children's Books, checklist no. 75.
Pale brown wrappers. [R & D 371]
Notes: Published in August 1895.

76. Poster to advertise T. Fisher Unwin's Pseudonym and Autonym Libraries.
[1894].
By Beardsley: Drawing of a standing woman with bookshop in distance,
adapted and colored from "Girl and a Bookshop," published in *Good Reading
About Many Books,* checklist no. 75A.
Color lithograph. [G 789; R 333; R & D 381; V 77]
Notes: One version headed "THE PSEUDONYM AND AUTONYM Libraries"
with book lists, two front covers, and publisher's name and address below.
"This poster was in use for some years after 1894 with varied letterpress; and
the design was adapted for a small advertisement slip…for the cover of Unwin's *Chap Book…*and for the front cover of *The Dream and the Business.*"[73]

[72] Described in caption as "Design for an Autonym Poster by Aubrey Beardsley."
[73] Reade 333. One version, reproducing the covers of the tenth edition of *Mademoiselle Ixe* by La-
noe Falconer [Mary Elizabeth Hawker] and *The Upper Berth* by F. Marion Crawford, has "W.
H. SMITH & SON, Printers. London, W.C. 3392694" at lower right below design. Another version, with book lists occupying a larger area, bears the imprint "UNWIN BROTHERS, LITHOS
LONDON, E.C." Vallance notes a version "reduced, printed in black, 6 copies only, on Japanese
vellum." Anthony d'Offay issued a facsimile of this poster; see footnote 29, page 26.

76A. Advertisement slip for T. Fisher Unwin's Pseudonym and Autonym Libraries. [1894?].
By Beardsley: Reduced size version of the poster to advertise T. Fisher Unwin's Pseudonym and Autonym Libraries, checklist no. 76.
Color lithograph.   [G 789; R & D 372; V 77]
Notes: Inserted in books and magazines published by Unwin, possibly even after the turn of the century.

76B. UNWIN'S CHAP BOOK. 1899–1900. London: Printed at the Gresham Press for T. Fisher Unwin, [1899].
By Beardsley: Front cover design adapted from poster to advertise T. Fisher Unwin's Pseudonym and Autonym Libraries, checklist no. 76.
Orange wrappers.   [R & D 373]
Notes: Includes works by Lewis Carroll, E. Nesbit, and S. R. Crockett.

76C. **John Oliver Hobbes [Pearl Mary-Teresa Craigie, née Richards]**
THE DREAM AND THE BUSINESS. London: T. Fisher Unwin, 1906.
By Beardsley: Front cover design in color (repeated on dust jacket) adapted from poster to advertise T. Fisher Unwin's Pseudonym and Autonym Libraries, checklist no. 76.
Cream cloth, dust jacket.   [G 789; R & D 374; V 77]
Notes: Published in August 1906. Copies denoted as from the "Colonial Edition" were issued in wrappers with the Beardsley design on front cover.

77. TO-DAY.[74] Special Winter Number, 17 November 1894.
By Beardsley: "Les Passades," full-page halftone reproduction. Reprinted in *The Idler,* March 1897.
Wrappers.   [G 944; R 332; R & D 464; V 100]

78. **Lucian**
LUCIAN'S TRUE HISTORY. Translated by Francis Hickes. Illustrated by William Strang, J. B. Clark, and Aubrey Beardsley. With an introduction by Charles Whibley. London: Privately printed,[75] 1894.
By Beardsley: Two drawings: "A Snare of Vintage" and "Dreams."

---

[74] Cover design by the artist Dudley Hardy. The issue's literary contents include "The Spectre of the Real" by Florence Henniker and Thomas Hardy, later incorporated into a Keynotes Series volume, *In Scarlet and Grey* (1896).
[75] *Lucian's True History* was in fact published by the firm of Lawrence and Bullen; see *Letters* p. 38.

Light green cloth (usually darkened to brown). 251 numbered copies.

By Beardsley: Additional illustration inserted, a platinotype (presumably by F. H. Evans) of a variant version of "A Snare of Vintage" printed on Japan vellum.[76] Reprinted in special issue of *The Uncollected Work,* checklist no. 177. Cream cloth. 54 numbered copies printed on Japan vellum.

Notes: Published in December 1894. The text was taken from Francis Hickes, *Certaine Select Dialogues of Lucian together with his True Historie, translated from the Greeke into English* (1634). In 1902 A. H. Bullen issued another edition of *Lucian's True History,* containing the two Beardsley illustrations published in 1894.[77] Two other drawings intended for *Lucian's True History* were published by Smithers in 1906 in *An Issue of Five Drawings Illustrative of Juvenal and Lucian,* checklist no. 149.[78]

79. **Joseph Pennell**
PEN DRAWING AND PEN DRAUGHTSMEN. Their work and their methods. A study of the art to-day with technical suggestions. London: Macmillan, 1894.
By Beardsley: Four drawings, including the previously unpublished "Portrait of Madame Réjane" [Gabrielle-Charlotte Réju].
Brown cloth.   [R & D 296; V 93]
Notes: Published in December 1894. Second edition of an 1889 work.

80. **[Edgar Allan Poe]**
[THE WORKS OF EDGAR ALLAN POE. Newly collected and edited, with a memoir, critical introductions, and notes by Edmund Clarence Stedman and George Edward Woodberry. The illustrations by Albert Edward Sterner. Chicago: Stone and Kimball, 1894–95].
By Beardsley: Four drawings: "The Murders in the Rue Morgue," "The Black Cat," "The Masque of the Red Death,"[79] and "The Fall of the House of Usher."

---

[76] Examples of this plate, though made for the special issue, are occasionally found inserted in ordinary paper copies. R & D 148 is a "proof" of the same design, described by W. G. Good: "This proof from a line-block is approximately the same size as the other illustrations to the book and the block was undoubtedly made with the intention of including the design among them."
[77] Gallatin p. 53.
[78] Vallance 74 III–IV describes an apparently different issue of these drawings: "Twenty copies of each were printed privately. One of them is unpublished; of the other, the upper portion was published in 'Later Work.' These illustrations were the earliest of the Artist's designs not intended for public circulation."
[79] Stone and Kimball used "The Masque of the Red Death" in *The Chap-Book,* 15 August 1894.

Loose plates printed on Japan vellum (size 5 × 3 ⅛ in.), without title-page or other indication of publication, in separate parchment-bound portfolio with cover design similar to the large paper and Japan paper "editions" of this ten-vol. set.[80]   [G 983–86, pp. 57–58; R 337–40; R & D 385–92; V 110]
Notes: In late December 1893 the Chicago publisher Stone and Kimball commissioned Beardsley to provide illustrations for the "Tales" section of the large paper version of Poe's collected works.[81] The four designs he completed appeared *not* in the volumes themselves, but in a separate, undated portfolio, about which there is uncertainty regarding the number of copies produced. In his authoritative history of the firm, Sidney Kramer makes no mention of this Beardsley portfolio, but does describe an entirely different (but identically bound) portfolio containing 18 engravings by mid-19th-century French artists. Kramer connects this to the Japan paper "edition" apparently reserved for the Poe set's collaborators and never offered for sale.[82] Gallatin at first believed that the Beardsley portfolio formed part of the large paper issue (250 copies on handmade paper) but later, in the Princeton catalogue he compiled with Alexander Wainwright, concluded that it "accompanied the Japan paper issue which consisted of only ten sets."[83] As evidence that Gallatin was correct, Warrack and Perkins cite the portfolio's scarcity; they located just six copies, including the one offered in their catalogue and others in the Gallatin collection at Princeton, and in the Victoria and Albert Museum.[84]

80A. FOUR ILLUSTRATIONS FOR THE TALES OF EDGAR ALLAN POE. Drawn by Aubrey Beardsley. Chicago: Herbert S. Stone, 1901.
By Beardsley: Four drawings reprinted from Stone and Kimball portfolio, checklist no. 80.
Loose plates (mounted on grey cardboard, reproduction size 8 ½ × 5 ½ in.) and separate text (16 pp., unpaged), all printed on Japan vellum in printed paper portfolio.   [G p. 58; R 337–40; R & D 389–92]
Notes: Published 28 December 1901. 250 numbered copies.

---

[80] Cover design by Frank Hazenplug (1873–?, who shortened his name to "Hazen" in 1910), a Stone and Kimball artist much influenced by Beardsley and famed for his *Chap-Book* posters.
[81] *Letters* p. 60. Stone and Kimball first advertised that the set would contain eight illustrations by Beardsley, then reduced the number to four.
[82] Kramer pp. 219–21. The first three vols., though dated 1894 on the title-pages and copyrighted that year, were not published until January 1895; the others appeared at intervals between April 1895 and March 1896. Presumably the portfolio was issued sometime during this period.
[83] Gallatin p. 57; A. E. Gallatin and Alexander Wainwright, *The Gallatin Beardsley Collection in the Princeton University Library*, checklist no. 193, p. 26.
[84] Warrack and Perkins 45, where the front cover of the portfolio is reproduced. Further analysis can be found in Charles Gullans and John Espey, "More Addenda to Kramer's *Stone & Kimball*," *PBSA* (1988), pp. 360–62.

80B. AUBREY BEARDSLEY'S DRAWINGS TO ILLUS-
TRATE THE TALES OF EDGAR ALLAN POE. With a portrait
of the artist. New York and Pittsburg [*sic*]: The Colonial Company, [1903?].
By Beardsley: Four drawings reprinted (same size) from Stone's 1901 portfo-
lio, checklist no. 80A.
Loose mounted plates in brown printed wrappers. [G p. 58]
Notes: Dated to "c. 1895" by Gallatin, to "about 1912" by Kramer,[85] and to
"around 1905" by others,[86] but most likely issued in 1903 to accompany the
Colonial Company's reissue of the set of Poe's *Works*.[87] The portfolio also
contains a portrait of Beardsley.

80C. ILLUSTRATIONS TO EDGAR ALLEN [*sic*] POE
FROM DRAWINGS BY AUBREY BEARDSLEY. Indianapolis:
Privately printed for the Aubrey Beardsley Club, 1926.
By Beardsley: Four drawings reprinted from earlier portfolios, along with 13
of the forgeries published by H. S. Nichols in 1920, see checklist no. 222.
Black cloth, dust jacket. [G p. 58]
Notes: 107 numbered copies. The issuer's name and place of publication are
decidedly fictitious and the limitation number probably meaningless.

81. TO-DAY. Spring Number, 1895.[88]
By Beardsley: "La Femme Incomprise." Reprinted in *The Idler*, March 1897,
checklist no. 114.
Wrappers. [G 213; R 252; V 46]

82. **John Davidson**
A FULL AND TRUE ACCOUNT OF THE WONDERFUL
MISSION OF EARL LAVENDER. Which lasted one night and one
day. With a history of the pursuit of Earl Lavender and Lord Brumm by
Mrs. Scamler and Maud Emblem. With a frontispiece by Aubrey Beardsley.
London: Ward & Downey, 1895.
By Beardsley: Frontispiece.
Blue cloth. [G 971; R 383; R & D supp. 431A; V 124]
Notes: Published in February 1895. Copies from a secondary binding-up lack
the publisher's name at foot of spine.

---

[85] Kramer p. 346.
[86] Warrack and Perkins 46.
[87] Gullans and Espey, "More Addenda to Kramer's *Stone & Kimball*," p. 362.
[88] *Letters* p. 46, note 2. The drawing was executed ca. March 1893.

83. Invitation card for John Lane's "Smoke" to meet Francis Elgar, President of the Sette of Odd Volumes, on 22 February 1895.
By Beardsley: Drawing (seated pierrot smoking, a copy of Vol. IV of *The Yellow Book* next to him) reproduced on second of two cards. Reprinted in *The Studio,* Vol. V, No. 30, September 1895.   [G 873; R 382; R & D 435; V 115]
Notes: The first card prints the text of the invitation. A number of alterations were made when the drawing was reprinted in *The Early Work,* checklist no. 133, including the removal of the letters "o" and "v" and the engraver's initials.

84. **Ola Hansson**
YOUNG OFEG'S DITTIES. Translated from the Swedish by George Egerton. London: John Lane, 1895.
By Beardsley: Front cover and title-page design.
Red cloth.   [G 843; R 315; R & D 370; V 125]
Notes: Published 26 February 1895. The format is similar to the volumes in Lane's Keynotes Series. In this case the title-page design is stamped in blind (in reverse) on the front cover.

85. THE HOUR. 27 March 1895.
By Beardsley: "Portrait of the Artist." Reprinted in *The Sun,* 28 March 1895, in *The Magazine of Art,* November 1896, and in *Reconsidering Aubrey Beardsley,* checklist no. 214.
Wrappers.   [G 869; V 111]
Notes: This is a variant version of another outline self-portrait, published in *Posters in Miniature,* checklist no. 108.

86. THE SKETCH. Vol. IX, No. 115, 10 April 1895.
By Beardsley: Two drawings, in interview with Beardsley entitled "An Apostle of the Grotesque": "A Child Standing by Its Mother's Bed" and "The Scarlet Pastorale."
Cream wrappers.   [G 870–71; R 384; R & D 465; V 112–13]

86A. THE LONDON YEAR BOOK. London: Grosvenor Press, 1898.
By Beardsley: Two drawings in article, "Aubrey Beardsley, Who Died March the Sixteenth, 1898" by W[illiam]. L[awler]., plus "The Scarlet Pastorale," printed in scarlet and white for the first time.
Brown cloth.   [R 384; R & D 465]

87. **Henry Thornton Wharton**
SAPPHO. Memoir, text, selected renderings, and a literal translation. London: John Lane, 1895.
By Beardsley: Front cover design.
Blue cloth.   [G 952; R 385; R & D 433; V 140]
Notes: Published in July 1895. The third edition of the book (originally published in 1885), the first in this format. A reprint, published by Lane in 1898, incorporates a "Memoir of Mr. H. T. Wharton" by J. S. Cotton.

88. ST. PAUL'S. 20 July 1895.
By Beardsley: "Pierrot and Cat" (drawn in 1893). Reprinted in the 2 April 1898 issue of the same magazine and in Gallatin.
Wrappers.   [G 282; R 294; R & D 287]

89. **Atey Nyne**[89]
WILMOT'S CHILD. By Atey Nyne, student and bachelor. London: T. Fisher Unwin, 1895.
By Beardsley: Front cover design adapted from poster to advertise T. Fisher Unwin's Children's Books, checklist no. 75.
Dark brown cloth-backed greyish-brown boards (also issued in wrappers).
Notes: Published in September 1895. A volume in Unwin's Autonym Library Series. The use of the Beardsley design was apparently first noted in a description of a copy offered in Bertram Rota cat. 64, *Books at Bodley House* (1940), item 871.

90. CATALOGUE OF RARE BOOKS OFFERED FOR SALE BY LEONARD SMITHERS. No. 3, September 1895. London: Leonard Smithers, 1895.
By Beardsley: Front cover design (faun reading to a woman).
Pale blue wrappers.   [G 949; R & D 514; V 121]
Notes: The same design was used for Smithers's catalogue No. 4, November 1895, bound in cream wrappers [R & D 515].

91. THE STUDIO. Vol. VI, No. 31, October 1895.
By Beardsley: "Isolde," color lithograph, in article "The Herkomer School."
Wrappers.   [G 987; R 392; V 119]

---

[89] Identified by the Library of Congress catalogue as Joseph Parker (1830–1902), a Congregationalist preacher, religious writer, and novelist (*Tyne Chylde* [1889] and *Paterson's Parish* [1898]).

92. Poster to advertise *The Spinster's Scrip*. [November? 1895].
By Beardsley: Drawing of two women, one holding a dog leash.
Line block.   [R 380; R & D 382]
Notes: "SOLD HERE" appears at upper left and information about book, price, and publisher in panel below.[90] *The Spinster's Scrip*, a volume of "daily extracts concerning matrimony," "compiled by" Cecil Raynor, was published by William Heinemann, London, in December 1895. The design for the poster was first published in *The New Review*, July 1894, checklist no. 71, as an illustration to "The Art of the Hoarding." A slightly different version of the design, incorporating a dog, appeared later in *The Early Work*, checklist no. 133.

93. **Charles Hiatt**
PICTURE POSTERS. A short history of the illustrated placard. With many reproductions of the most artistic examples in all countries. London: George Bell and Sons, 1895.
By Beardsley: Designs for the Avenue Theatre poster, checklist no. 62, and for the poster to advertise *The Yellow Book*, checklist no. 65F.
Light green cloth.
Notes: Published in November 1895.

94. **Walt Ruding**[91]
AN EVIL MOTHERHOOD. An impressionist novel. Frontispiece by Aubrey Beardsley. London: Elkin Mathews, 1896.
By Beardsley: Frontispiece.
Dark blue cloth.

FIRST ISSUE   [G 976; R 394; R & D 431; V 136]
"Black Coffee" frontispiece (halftone) glued in.

SECOND ISSUE   [G 975; R 395; R & D 432; V 135]
"Portrait of the Author" substitute frontispiece (line block) glued in.

THIRD (REMAINDER) ISSUE
"Portrait of the Author" glued in, "Black Coffee" inserted or tipped in.

Notes: John Lane objected to his former partner's and artist's use of "Black Coffee"—a drawing (also known as "Café Noir") originally produced for the ill-fated Vol. v of *The Yellow Book*—for the frontispiece to this curious novel.

---

[90] Anthony d'Offay issued a facsimile of this poster; see footnote 29, page 26.
[91] In two inscribed copies of the book, one from the "first issue" presented to the journalist and reviewer Mrs. Beer on 7 November 1895 (Colbeck, Vol. 1, p. 41), the other from the "second issue" given on 14 November 1895 to the volume's publisher, Elkin Mathews, the author signed his name "Walter Ruding."

Beardsley immediately provided a substitute design,[92] the "Portrait of the Author," which may or may not depict the mysterious Ruding (who may or may not really have existed).[93] It is said that only six (or 12) "review copies" were issued with "Black Coffee" bound in,[94] but the design was by no means "suppressed"—the plate being found, along with the substitute frontispiece, in a "remainder" issued perhaps several years later. The first edition of 1,000 copies was published in November 1895 with a postdated title-page. A variant of the book is known marked "Second Thousand" on the verso of the half-title with the additional imprint of George H. Richmond & Co., New York on title-page and "G. H. Richmond & Co." superimposed over "Elkin Mathews 1896" at foot of spine.

95. **Joseph Pennell**
MODERN ILLUSTRATION. London: G. Bell and Sons, 1895.
By Beardsley: "La Comédie aux Enfers." Reprinted (in a larger sized halftone) in *A Second Book of Fifty Drawings*, checklist no. 132.   [G 854; V 61]

ORDINARY ISSUE
Green cloth, dust jacket.

LARGE PAPER ISSUE
Parchment wrappers. 125 numbered copies printed on Japan vellum.

Notes: Published in December 1895.

96. CATALOGUE OF RARE BOOKS OFFERED FOR SALE BY LEONARD SMITHERS. No. 5, 1896. London: Leonard Smithers, 1896.
By Beardsley: Front cover design (woman reading on a sofa).
Pink wrappers.   [G 950; R 402; R & D 516; V 145]
Notes: Published probably in late 1895 since the inside covers contain an announcement for the first number of *The Savoy*, checklist no. 103. The same design was used for two further Smithers catalogues of rare books dated simply "1896": No. 6, bound in light blue wrappers and issued in the period

---

[92] *Letters* p. 104.
[93] Reade and Dickinson 432 succinctly note, "No other titles by this author are recorded." The only "proof" of Ruding's existence known to me consists of the inscribed copies of the book mentioned in note 91 above and Beardsley's request, in January 1896, for the publisher to send him a copy of "Mr. Ruding's book" (*Letters* pp. 110–11). As with so many writers of the 1890s, the name may be a pseudonym.
[94] Vallance 136 asserts that "Black Coffee" (to which he gives the alternate title "Café Noir") was "bound up in six review copies only, and then recalled." G 976 repeats the statement, as does R & D 431; the "first issue" copy described in the last also bears the publisher's bookplate.

January–March 1896 [R & D 517], and No. 7, in violet-grey wrappers, issued prior to July 1896 [R & D 518].[95] It was later adapted for the cover of at least one of John Lane's catalogues of publications and also for Elkin Mathews's catalogue 42, *Books of the Nineties* [1932], which offered the original drawing (item 12) for £105.

97. A LONDON GARLAND. Selected from five centuries of English verse by W. E. Henley.[96] With pictures by members of the Society of Illustrators. London: Macmillan, 1895.
By Beardsley: Illustration to "At a Distance,"[97] poem by Justin Huntly McCarthy. Reprinted with the title "A Suggested Reform in Ballet Costume" in *A Second Book of Fifty Drawings,* checklist no. 132.

ORDINARY ISSUE
Cream linen, top edge gilt.   [G 867; R 396; R & D 467; V 108]

SPECIAL ISSUE
Cream parchment, all edges gilt.[98]

Notes: Published in December 1895. Half-title, initial letters, and cover design by Alfred Parsons.

98. H[enry]. D[uff]. Traill
THE BARBAROUS BRITISHERS. A tip-top novel. London: John Lane, [1896].
By Beardsley: Front cover and title-page design and key monogram (found on back cover and verso of title-page), mimicking the artist's designs for Grant Allen's Keynotes Series volume, *The British Barbarians: A Hill-Top Novel,* checklist no. 45, of which this work is a parody.
Brown wrappers.   [G 860; R 316; R & D 375–77; V 70]
Notes: Published in January 1896. There are two binding variants, one with the design printed in dark green, the other in dark brown. The woman caricatured in Beardsley's design is thought to be the actress Ada Lundberg.

---

[95] Bertram Rota cat. 150 (1967), item 123, points out—in a description of a seemingly complete collection of Smithers's rare book catalogues, nos. 1–14 (1895–98) that there are two issues of catalogue no. 7, "the first published from Arundel Street, the second overstamped with the Royal Arcade address." The move was made in September 1896. It does not appear, contrary to R 402, that Beardsley provided the cover design for any of the catalogues before no. 3, September 1895.
[96] Henley chose the literary contents; the anonymous selection of illustrations was done by Joseph Pennell, according to his inscription in a copy in the Pennell Collection at the Library of Congress.
[97] Described by R & D as "showing a ballet dancer in a costume as prescribed by Mrs. Grundy."
[98] For details of the two bindings see Colbeck, Vol. 1, p. 366.

99. **H[enry]. de Vere Stacpoole**[99]
    PIERROT! A story. London: John Lane, 1896.
    By Beardsley: Front cover, back cover, spine, title-page, and endpaper de-
    signs—repeated in the three subsequent volumes in the series, the covers
    printed in different colors.[100]   [G 1044–49, pp. 64–65; R 397–401;
                                                    R & D 449–52; V 141]
    Buff cloth printed in red.   [R & D 454]
    Notes: Vol. I of Pierrot's Library. Published in January 1896. Beardsley re-
    ceived £15 for all the designs.[101]

100. **Mrs. Egerton Castle [Agnes Sweetman Castle]**
    MY LITTLE LADY ANNE. London: John Lane, 1896.
    By Beardsley: Front cover, back cover, spine, title-page, and endpaper designs,
    from *Pierrot!*, checklist no. 99.
    Buff cloth printed in blue.   [R & D 458]
    Notes: Vol. II of Pierrot's Library. Published in May 1896.

101. **A. T. G. Price**
    SIMPLICITY. London: John Lane, 1896.
    By Beardsley: Front cover, back cover, spine, title-page, and endpaper designs,
    from *Pierrot!*, checklist no. 99.
    Buff cloth printed in green.   [R & D 455–56]
    Notes: Vol. III of Pierrot's Library. Published in October 1896.

102. **Vincent Brown**
    MY BROTHER. London: John Lane, 1896.
    By Beardsley: Front cover, back cover, spine, title-page, and endpaper designs,
    from *Pierrot!*, checklist no. 99.
    Buff cloth printed in brown.   [R & D 459]
    Notes: Vol. IV of Pierrot's Library. Published in October 1896.

---

[99] (1863–1951), Dublin-born physician turned author, amateur scientist and undersea explorer.
"Qualifying in 1891, Stacpoole signed on as a ship's doctor and travelled all over the world, ex-
periences which he later used in his novels," including his 1908 bestseller, *The Blue Lagoon* (John
Sutherland, *The Stanford Companion to Victorian Fiction* [1989], p. 600). Another title by
Stacpoole, *Death, The Knight, and the Lady,* announced as "forthcoming" in Pierrot's Library, was
eventually published by John Lane (1897) in a different format without the Beardsley designs.
[100] Gallatin and Vallance list the designs but neglect to give the titles of the books or to say how
many were published in the series.
[101] *Letters* p. 94.

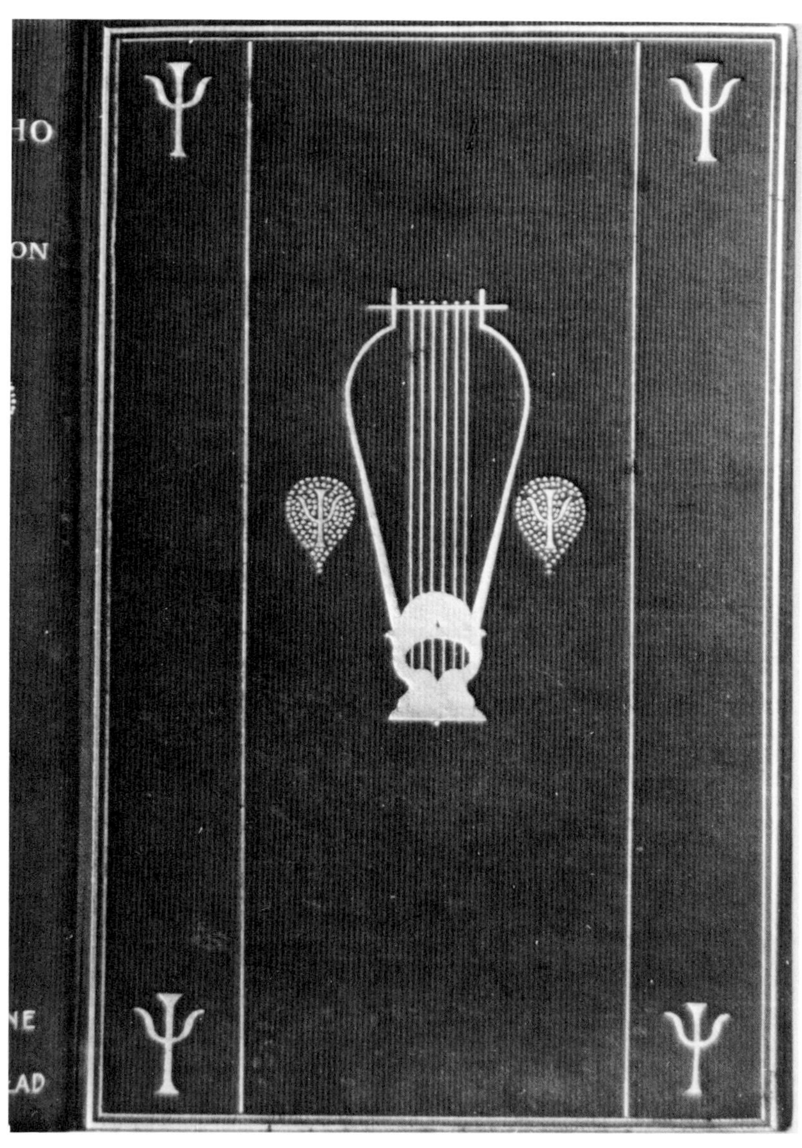

Henry Thornton Wharton, *Sappho. Memoir, text, selected renderings, and a literal translation*. London: John Lane, 1895. Front cover. [checklist no. 87]

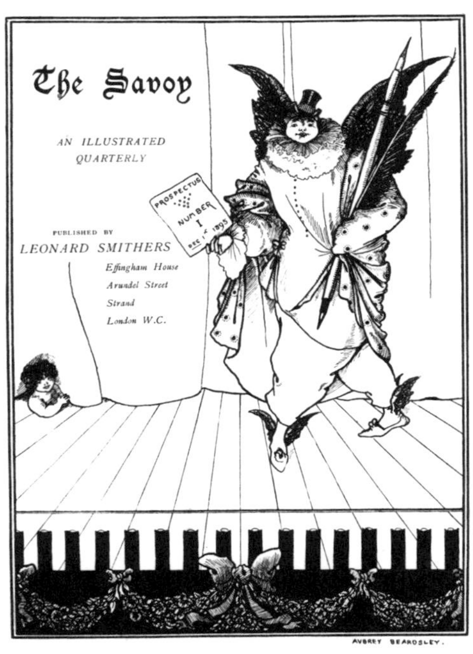

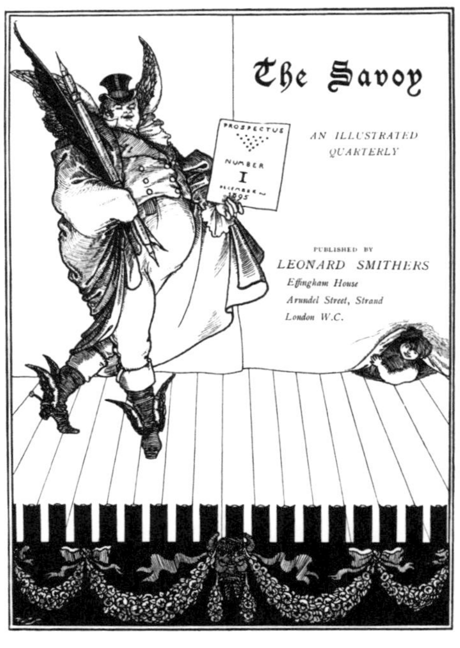

Prospectuses for *The Savoy,*
November 1895
[checklist no. 103A]

Front covers
Above: "Pierrot" version
Right: "John Bull" version

103. THE SAVOY. Nos. 1–8. London: Leonard Smithers, 1896. (Nos. 1–2 as a quarterly, January and April 1896; nos. 3–8 as a monthly, July–December 1896). [G pp. 58–62]

NO. 1, January 1896.   [G 989–99; R 415–26; R & D 528; V 146 V–XVI]
By Beardsley: Seven drawings, front cover design,[102] back cover design (publisher's "Siegfried" device), title-page design (repeated in No. 2), contents leaf preceding lists of contents, and separately printed Christmas card (usually tipped-in, sometimes loosely inserted). Also contains Beardsley's poem, "The Three Musicians," and chapters I–III of his novel, "Under the Hill."[103]
Pink boards.
Notes: Published 11 January 1896.

NO. 2, April 1896.   [G 1000–3; R 427–30; R & D 529; V 146 XVII–XX]
By Beardsley: Four drawings (including "A Footnote," a self-portrait), front cover design, back cover design (publisher's "Siegfried" device), and title-page design (repeated from No. 1). Contains chapter IV of "Under the Hill."
Pink boards.
Notes: Published ca. 24–25 April 1896. 3,000 copies. Extra prints of the front covers of Nos. 1 and 2 are bound in before the advertisements at back.[104] According to Reade and Dickinson there were two issues: in the first the title-page leaf is integral and has the imprint of the Chiswick Press on verso, in the second the leaf is a cancel and the verso is blank.[105]

NO. 3, July 1896.   [G 1004–7; R 431–34; R & D 530; V 146 XXI–XXIV]
By Beardsley: Two drawings, front cover design (repeated on first preliminary leaf), and title-page design (publisher's "Puck on Pegasus" device, repeated in reduced size on back cover). Also contains Beardsley's poem, "The Ballad of a Barber."
Light blue-green wrappers.
Notes: Published ca. 22 June 1896. 3,000 copies. Title-page and back cover designs used in all subsequent issues of the magazine.

---

[102] "Proofs" [R & D 527] of Beardsley's original design for the front cover [G 989; R 416], showing a child urinating on a copy of *The Yellow Book*, are relatively common, despite the statement, made by Gallatin and others, that they were "suppressed."
[103] This opening section of "Under the Hill" was parodied by Ada Leverson in "Dickens Up to Date," *Punch* (25 January 1896).
[104] "For the convenience of such subscribers as desire to bind up 'The Savoy' into volumes, is appended a print of the covers of Nos. 1 and 2, pulled on white paper, which may be bound in, in substitution for the pink cardboard covers." (Publisher's Note, p. 197). In the collected issue in three vols. bound by the publisher the two substitute cover leaves are moved from the end of No. 2 to their proper locations preceding the half-titles of Nos. 1 and 2.
[105] All the issues of the magazine, with the exception of No. 1, which bears the imprint of Smithers's one-time partner H. S. Nichols, were printed by the Chiswick Press.

NO. 4, August 1896.   [G 1008; R 435; R & D 531; V 146 XXV]
By Beardsley: Front cover design (repeated on first preliminary leaf) and title-page design (publisher's "Puck on Pegasus" device, repeated on back cover).
Light blue-green wrappers.
Notes: Published ca. 24 July 1896. 2,400 copies.

NO. 5, September 1896.   [G 1009–10; R 436–37; R & D 532;
                                              V 146 XXVI-XXVII]
By Beardsley: One drawing, front cover design[106] (repeated on first preliminary leaf), and title-page design (publisher's "Puck on Pegasus" device, repeated on back cover).
Light blue-green wrappers.
Notes: Published ca. 28 August 1896. 1,500 copies.

NO. 6, October 1896.   [G 1011–12; R 438–39; R & D 533;
                                              V 146 XXVIII-XXIX]
By Beardsley: One drawing, front cover design (repeated on first preliminary leaf), and title-page design (publisher's "Puck on Pegasus" device, repeated on back cover).
Light blue-green wrappers.
Notes: Published ca. 29 September 1896. 1,500 copies.

NO. 7, November 1896.   [G 1013–15; R 440–41; R & D 534;
                                              V 146 XXX-XXXII]
By Beardsley: Two drawings, front cover design (repeated on first preliminary leaf), and title-page design (publisher's "Puck on Pegasus" device, repeated on back cover). Also contains translation of Catullus's "Carmen CI."[107]
Light blue-green wrappers.
Notes: Published ca. 30 October 1896. 1,500 copies.

NO. 8, December 1896.   [G 1016–27; R 442–53; R & D 535;
                                              V 146 XXXIII-XLIV]
By Beardsley: 12 drawings (including four for "The Comedy of the Rhinegold"[108]), front cover design (repeated on first preliminary leaf), and title-page design (publisher's "Puck on Pegasus" device, repeated on back cover).
Light blue-green wrappers.
Notes: Published ca. 13 December 1896. 1,500 copies.

---

[106] Gallatin 1009 notes, "Signed, for a practical joke, Giulio Floriani." See R 436.

[107] This translation has been set to music (voice and piano) by the composer Ned Rorem (born 1923) and published under the title "Catullus, on the burial of his brother," by Boosey & Hawkes, New York, in 1969. According to a photocopy (New York Public Library) of the original manuscript score, the song was written in Philadelphia, 6–7 May 1947.

[108] In September 1896 Beardsley wrote to Smithers that he was "writing an elaborate version of *Das Rheingold,* called *The Comedy of the Rhinegold*" based on Wagner's opera (*Letters* p. 164 and note 2 on p. 165). This project never materialized. See G 1020–23 and R 446.

By Beardsley: On all three volumes: new front cover (adapted from title-page for No. 1) and spine designs; back cover design repeats publisher's "Puck on Pegasus" device.

Three vols. Violet cloth (some sets in vellum, with cloth covers bound in).[109]　　　　　　　[G 1028 and pp. 58–59; R & D 536–37, V 146 XLV]
Notes: Published in late November or early December 1896. In No. 7 the editor, Arthur Symons, wrote, "I have to announce that with the next number, completing a year's existence, the present issue of 'The Savoy' will come to an end….We therefore retire from the arena, not entirely dissatisfied if not a trifle disappointed, leaving to those who care for it our year's work, which will be presented to you in three volumes, in a cover of Mr. Beardsley's designing."[110] Three variant cloth bindings are recorded. The first has "Leonard Smithers 1896" at the foot of the spine, the second "Leonard Smithers & Co.," representing the change in the publisher's status in about 1897. The third has "John Lane" on the spine and the name of Leonard Smithers removed from the covers, presumably indicating a tertiary binding-up after Smithers's bankruptcy, when Lane took over his Beardsley publications.[111]

103A. Prospectus for *The Savoy.* November 1895.
By Beardsley: Front cover and back cover (publisher's "Siegfried" device) designs, and initial "A."[112]　　　　　　　[G 1031–32; R 415; V 146 III–IV]
Pink wrappers (some copies with inserted card offering trade discount).

"PIERROT" VERSION　　　　　　　　　　　　[G 1030 and p. 62; V 146 I]
Front cover design with Pierrot at right (holding in right hand flyer reading "PROSPECTUS NUMBER I DEC I^st 1895"), child peeking out from underneath curtain at left. Reprinted (without letterpress) in *The Best of Beardsley,* checklist no. 189.

---

[109] The precise status of the vellum-bound sets, of which very few are known to exist, is unclear. Smithers's contemporary announcements do not advertise the availability of such copies, and there is no mention of them in Vallance or in the other early literature on Beardsley. Two of the surviving sets may have been specially produced. One, described in Gordon N. Ray, *The Illustrator and the Book in England from 1700 to 1914* (1976), item 317, p. 197—containing various pieces of ephemera—was bound by Riviere; another, R & D 539–41, belonged to Beardsley's patron Herbert Charles Pollitt and may also have been made to order.
[110] Arthur Symons, "Editorial Note," *The Savoy,* No. 7 (November 1896), p. 7. A publisher's slip dated October 1896, announcing the demise of the magazine and the availability of the three-volume collected issue (price one guinea), is found in some copies of No. 7 (and possibly No. 6).
[111] J. Stephan Lawrence, Rare Books, *Catalogue Number 44: Aubrey Beardsley,* checklist no. 206, item 104 argues that copies of the third variety—with Lane's name on the spine—represent a "trial binding." Certainly they are most uncommon. A copy has been seen in the Smithers binding with the pink boards and light blue-green wrappers from the separate numbers bound in.
[112] *Letters* p. 98, note 1 speculates that this initial was "probably intended" for Beardsley's poem, "The Three Musicians," published in No. 1 of *The Savoy.*

"JOHN BULL" VERSION [G 1029 and p. 62; R 414; R & D 538; V 146 11]
Front cover design with John Bull at left (holding in left hand flyer reading "PROSPECTUS NUMBER 1 DECEMBER 1895"), child peeking out from underneath curtain at right. Reprinted (without letterpress) in *The Best of Beardsley*, checklist no. 189.[113] The basic design was also used for the contents leaf preceding lists of literary and art contents in No. 1 of the magazine.

Notes: There are two distinct prospectuses for *The Savoy*, each with a different Beardsley design on the front cover. Of the several and varying explanations, that of Bernard Shaw (a contributor to the magazine) is the most plausible: "It was not the *cover* of the *Savoy* that made the trouble, but the preliminary pictorial circular. Beardsley made a charming design of a Pierrot stepping out on the stage to announce the paper. Smithers foolishly objected that it suggested flippancy and that John Bull would like something serious. Beardsley revenged himself by substituting a monumental John Bull for the Pierrot. Eighty thousand of this were circulated before George Moore's scrutiny detected that John had been represented in a condition of strained sexual excitement. All the contributors therefore met and informed Smithers that he must 'withdraw' the circular. Not having any of the 80,000 left he agreed; and peace was restored."[114] It seems that by the time of Moore's protest (late November 1895) the "Pierrot" version had already been printed, the copies either distributed or—given Smithers's methods—retained for sale as "suppressed" Beardsleyana.[115] The whole wrangle delayed publication of *The Savoy*, which, as both prospectuses state, was scheduled to appear in December 1895 (to take advantage of the Christmas market).

103B. Poster to advertise *The Savoy*. [mid-November 1896].
By Beardsley: Adapted from front cover design for *The Savoy*, No. 8, December 1896, with color and background lines added by the artist.[116]
Color lithograph.   [G p. 62; R 453; R & D 548]

[113] Front cover design also used for a "bookseller's window card" on thicker paper; see J. Stephan Lawrence, Rare Books, *Catalogue Number 44: Aubrey Beardsley*, checklist no. 206, item 107.
[114] Quoted in Grant Richards, *Author Hunting* (1934), note on p. 19. On 28 November 1895 Shaw wrote to Charles Charrington, "...I am in the thick of this Beardsley business, the post of fighting man in chief having been conceded to me with unanimity by the scandalised contributors" (Bernard Shaw, *Collected Letters, 1874–1897*, ed. Dan H. Laurence [1865], p. 572). For an authoritative discussion of the entire imbroglio, see Karl Beckson, *Arthur Symons: A Life* (1987), pp. 123–24.
[115] Reade and Dickinson 538 suggest this when they write (speaking in error of the "John Bull" version) that "it was not sent out therefore and considerable numbers remained in the publisher's stock." A proof copy of the Pierrot prospectus bearing Smithers's manuscript corrections and annotations is in the author's collection.
[116] Beardsley produced the lithograph by adding pen and ink and watercolor to pulls of the line block supplied to him by Smithers in October 1896. See *Letters* pp. 187–88.

Notes: Promotes the collected issue of the magazine in three volumes, price one guinea.[117] The legend "c.f. kell, printer, 8, furnival street, london, e.c." is printed below the design.

104. **Robert B[ruce]. Douglas**
THE LIFE AND TIMES OF MADAME DU BARRY. London: Leonard Smithers, 1896.
By Beardsley: Front cover design.
Violet cloth.   [G 1053; R 456; R & D 553, 578; V 152]
Notes: Published in April 1896. There are apparently several variants, with copies found in both vertically and horizontally ribbed cloth, the latter described by Reade and Dickinson as lacking the Dutch printer's imprint on verso of title-page.

105. **Alexander Pope**
THE RAPE OF THE LOCK. An heroi-comical poem in five cantos. Embroidered with nine drawings by Aubrey Beardsley. London: Leonard Smithers, 1896.
By Beardsley: Eight illustrations,[118] frontispiece, and front cover design.[119]
[G 1033–42; R 403–12; R & D 505–8; V 144]

ORDINARY ISSUE   [G pp. 62–63; R & D 511, 513]
Turquoise blue cloth. 1,000 copies printed on wove paper, produced in two impressions of 500 each, in August and December 1896.
Notes: A secondary binding (probably used for the second 500) in bright blue cloth with "Leonard Smithers and Co." on the spine has been reported.

SPECIAL ISSUE   [G pp. 62–63; R & D 509]
Vellum. 25 numbered copies printed on Japan vellum (some not numbered).[120]

Notes: Published between 23 April and early May 1896. A paperback facsimile was published by Dover Publications, New York, in 1968.

105A. ["BIJOU" EDITION]. Embroidered with eleven drawings by Aubrey Beardsley. London: Leonard Smithers, 1897.
By Beardsley: Eight illustrations, frontispiece, and front cover design from first edition, checklist no. 105, reproduced on reduced size plates, with new cover design (reproduced also on plate). [G 1043 and p. 64; R 413; V p. 102]

---

[117] Anthony d'Offay issued a facsimile of this poster; see footnote 29, page 26.
[118] One illustration, "The Rape of the Lock," was reproduced on the book's prospectus [G p. 64].
[119] Front covers of both issues of the first edition and of the "Bijou" edition are conveniently reproduced in Simon Wilson, *Beardsley,* checklist no. 205A, Pl. 47; see also R 403.
[120] The Chiswick Press records state that in fact 37 copies were printed on Japan vellum, 25 of which were for sale.

ORDINARY ISSUE   [R 413; R & D 510]
Red cloth. 1,000 copies printed on art paper.

SPECIAL ISSUE
Vellum. 50 copies printed on Japan vellum, numbered and initialed by Smithers.

Notes: Published ca. 4 August 1896 with postdated title-page.

105B. [SECOND "BIJOU" EDITION]. With illustrations by Aubrey Beardsley. London: John Lane, 1902.
By Beardsley: Eight illustrations and frontispiece from first edition, checklist no. 105.
Olive green cloth, orange dust jacket.   [G p. 64; R & D 512; V p. 102]
Notes: Published in September 1901 with postdated title-page. Vol. x of Lane's Flowers of Parnassus Series edited by F. B. Money-Coutts. Copies were also issued in green leather. Lane published a second edition in 1916.

105C. DER LOCKENRAUB. Ein komisches heldengedicht von Alexander Pope. Mit neun zeichnungen von A. Beardsley. Leipzig: Insel-Verlag, 1908.
By Beardsley: Eight illustrations, frontispiece, and front cover design from first edition, checklist no. 105.
Black boards.

ORDINARY ISSUE
Nos. 101–800 of 800 numbered copies printed on Holland paper.

SPECIAL ISSUE
Nos. 1–100 of 800 numbered copies printed on Japan vellum.

Notes: Translation (by Rudolf A. Schröder).

106. **Ernest Dowson**
VERSES. London: Leonard Smithers, 1896.
By Beardsley: Front cover design.[121] Reused for *The Poems of Ernest Dowson,* checklist no. 146.   [G 954; R 457; R & D 554; V 148]

[121] Upon receiving copies of *Verses* in early June 1896, Dowson told Smithers, "My compliments and thanks for the luxury with which you have encadré my lucubrations. The cover is really very beautiful: and I congratulate Beardsley if, as I gather, his is the design," adding, a few days later, that "Beardsley's binding block is admirable—*simplex munditiis,* & yet most sumptuous" (Ernest Dowson, *The Letters of Ernest Dowson,* ed. Desmond Flower and Henry Maas [1967], p. 365).

Imitation parchment. 300 copies printed on Van Gelder paper.

LARGE PAPER ISSUE
Imitation parchment. 30 numbered copies printed on Japan vellum.[122]

Notes: Published probably in late May or very early June 1896 (June, according to *The English Catalogue*). Copies from the primary binding have "Leonard Smithers 1896" at foot of spine. One of the book's poems, "Soli Cantare Periti Arcades," is dedicated "For Aubrey Beardsley."

107. **Aristophanes**
THE LYSISTRATA OF ARISTOPHANES. Now first wholly translated into English and illustrated with eight full-page drawings by Aubrey Beardsley. London: [Leonard Smithers], 1896.
By Beardsley: Eight illustrations.
Blue boards, printed label on cover.   [G 1066–73 and p. 67; R 460–67;
                                          R & D 461–63, 466; V 143]
Notes: Issued in October 1896. 100 numbered copies with manuscript limitation statement.[123] A variant, not numbered and bound in boards covered with grey-blue laid paper, has been noted (Warrack and Perkins 69). The anonymous translation was by Samuel Smith (1867–1938), an Oxford friend of Ernest Dowson's who became a schoolmaster.

107A. [ANOTHER EDITION]. [Vienna:] Privatdruck, 1905.
By Beardsley: Eight illustrations from first edition, checklist no. 107.
Loose leaves in paper folder.   [G p. 67]
Notes: 400 copies. Copies are recorded with a ninth plate reproducing a Beardsley forgery.[124]

107B. [ANOTHER EDITION]. [Germany:] Privatdruck, 1905.
By Beardsley: Eight illustrations from first edition, checklist no. 107.
Loose leaves in yellow paper portfolio.   [Warrack and Perkins 70]
Notes: 100 numbered copies.

107C. [ANOTHER EDITION]. Illustrated by Aubrey Beardsley. London: Beardsley Press, 1927.
By Beardsley: Eight illustrations from first edition, checklist no. 107.
Silver cloth-backed black boards.   [G p. 67]

---

[122] Chiswick Press records show that 35 copies were actually produced, of which 30 were for sale.
[123] Gallatin claims that *Lysistrata* was published "in an edition of 150 copies, 50 being on large paper." No large paper copies have been located.
[124] Thomas G. Boss Fine Books, *Catalogue Five: The Turn of the Century, Part 1* [1991], item 15, where the limitation is stated to be 100 copies.

107D. [ANOTHER EDITION]. [London, ca. 1929].
By Beardsley: Eight illustrations from first edition, checklist no. 107.
Loose collotype plates in blue cloth portfolio. [R 467]
Notes: The reproductions are printed on paper watermarked "AB." Dated by
Reade to about 1925 but likely produced in 1929. R. A. Walker wrote an in-
troduction but this was not included when the portfolio was issued.

107E. [ANOTHER EDITION]. Wholly translated into English and
illustrated with eight full-page drawings by Aubrey Beardsley. With a preface
on Aristophanic comedy and its reflection in the art of the illustrator by
George Frederick Lees. Paris: Privately printed, 1931.
By Beardsley: Eight illustrations from first edition, checklist no. 107.
Folded leaves in cream wrappers, with plates in separate envelope, in slipcase.

ORDINARY ISSUE
500 numbered copies.

SPECIAL ISSUE
25 numbered copies printed on Van Gelder paper, with the plates on Japan
vellum.

107F. [ANOTHER EDITION]. Illustrated with eight full-page drawings by Aubrey Beardsley. London, 1896. [New York: Odyssey Publications,
1967].
By Beardsley: Eight illustrations from first edition, checklist no. 107.
Blue boards, printed label on front cover, slipcase.
Notes: 515 numbered copies (15 of which were not for sale). Photolitho-
graphic facsimile of the first edition, checklist no. 107, using paper and binding similar to the original. The publisher's name, information about the
edition, and a limitation notice are found on the verso of the title-page.

107G. [ANOTHER EDITION]. Illustrated by Aubrey Beardsley and
ancient Athenian artists. New York: Land's End Press, 1968.
Notes: Text translated by Jack Brussel.

107H. [ANOTHER EDITION]. Illustrated by Aubrey Beardsley. Lon-
don: Academy Editions, [1973].
By Beardsley: Eight illustrations from first edition, checklist no. 107.
Black cloth.
Notes: Co-published by St. Martin's Press, New York.

108. POSTERS IN MINIATURE. With an introduction by Edward Penfield. New York: R. H. Russell, 1896.
By Beardsley: Seven drawings and posters, one of which, a "Self-Portrait," is published for the first time. Reprinted in *The Early Work,* checklist no. 133.
Yellow cloth. [R 472; V 111]
Notes: A variant of the outline "Self Portrait" was reproduced in halftone in *The Hour,* 27 March 1895 and elsewhere, see checklist no. 84. Contains a foreword by Percival Pollard.

109. **Vincent O'Sullivan**
A BOOK OF BARGAINS. With a frontispiece by Aubrey Beardsley. London: Leonard Smithers, 1896.
By Beardsley: Frontispiece.
Plum cloth. [G 1052; R 475; R & D 561; V 153]
Notes: Published in November 1896. Author's first independent book. Copies from the primary binding have "Leonard Smithers 1896" at foot of spine, later copies "Leonard Smithers and Co. 1896." The publisher's "Puck on Pegasus" device is found on the title-page.

110. MR. LEONARD SMITHERS' LIST OF PUBLICATIONS. [London:] Leonard Smithers, [ca. November 1896].
By Beardsley: Front cover design (with letterpress) for *A Book of Fifty Drawings,* checklist no. 112.[125]
Sewn. [R 473]
Notes: This booklet—to be distinguished from Smithers's catalogues of rare books—advertises *The Savoy,* Max Beerbohm's *Caricatures of Twenty-Five Gentlemen* (with a caricature of Beardsley, published in December 1896), and various books illustrated by Beardsley and Charles Conder.

111. THE PARADE. An illustrated gift book for boys and girls. 1897. London: Henry, 1897.
By Beardsley: Title-page decoration (*not* the lettering).
Red cloth, dust jacket. [G 953; R 474; V 138]
Notes: Published in November 1896. Edited by Gleeson White, with contributions by Max Beerbohm, John Oliver Hobbes, Richard Le Gallienne, Laurence Housman, Charles Robinson, and others. The cover and endpaper designs are by Paul Woodroffe.

[125] See J. Stephan Lawrence, Rare Books, *Catalogue Number 44: Aubrey Beardsley,* checklist no. 206, item 116.

112. **Aubrey Beardsley**
A BOOK OF FIFTY DRAWINGS. With an iconography by Aymer
Vallance. London: Leonard Smithers, 1897.
By Beardsley: 50 drawings, five published for the first time including the tail-
piece (a silhouette self-portrait), front cover design, back cover design (pub-
lisher's "Puck on Pegasus" device, repeated on title-page[126]).   [R 473; V 154]

ORDINARY ISSUE   [G p. 73]
Red cloth. 500 copies.

LARGE PAPER ISSUE   [G p. 73; R & D 567]
Vellum. 50 copies printed on Japan vellum, numbered and signed by the
publisher.

Notes: Published in January 1897. Beardsley made the selection himself. Vallance's iconography, the first attempt to list the artist's works, was revised for
Robert Ross's *Aubrey Beardsley,* checklist no. 154.

113. Bookplate for Herbert Charles Pollitt.[127] [March 1897].
Adapted from the artist's own bookplate design, published in *A Book of Fifty
Drawings,* checklist no. 112. Legend reads "MR POLLITT'S BOOKPLATE."
Line block on thin paper.   [G 1065; R 471; R & D 551]
Notes: "Beardsley had been promising Pollitt a bookplate for some time.
When this drawing was published in A Book of Fifty Drawings in 1897 con-
science may have got the better of the artist and in Pollitt's copy of the edition
de luxe Beardsley added the lettering in india ink on the reproduction. From
this Pollitt had a new block made (by Carl Hentschel) for his own use."[128]

114. THE IDLER. Vol. XI, March 1897.
By Beardsley: 12 drawings, in "interview," "Mr. Aubrey Beardsley and his
Work," by Arthur H. Lawrence.[129]
Wrappers.

---

[126] Beardsley proposed "a little vignette of some sort" for the title-page but he "failed with this
drawing and Smithers used *Puck on Pegasus*" instead; see *Letters* p. 157 and note 2 on p. 158.
[127] (1871–1942), collector, amateur thespian, correspondent of Wilde, and patron of Beardsley
and Whistler. In 1907 he provided an essay for the Galeries Shirleys Beardsley exhibition catalogue, checklist no. 150.
[128] Warrack and Perkins 82. For further details see *Letters* pp. 263, 267, 276 and Steven Hobbs,
"Mr. Pollitt's Bookplate," *The Book Collector* (1987), pp. 518–30, where the original drawing
(made on 27 February 1897) in Pollitt's copy of *A Book of Fifty Drawings* is reproduced.
[129] *Letters* pp. 229 and 234. To Smithers Beardsley wrote on 20 December 1896: "This afternoon
I have been interviewing myself for *The Idler,* and hope I have not said too many foolish things."
In another letter, to Robert Ross, dated "[c. 25 December 1896]" he adds, "I want you to forgive
me for having plagiarized one or two of your good things you told me you had written in an
imaginary interview with me a long time ago. *The Idler* is publishing something about me from
notes of my own, and I stuck in boldly a few Robertian plums...."

115. **Ernest Dowson**
THE PIERROT OF THE MINUTE. A dramatic phantasy in one act. With a frontispiece, initial letter, vignette, and cul-de-lampe by Aubrey Beardsley. London: Leonard Smithers, 1897.
By Beardsley: Front cover design, back cover design (publisher's "Puck on Pegasus" device, repeated on title-page), frontispiece, initial letter, vignette, and cul-de-lampe (tailpiece).   [G 1079–83; R 476–79; R & D 556–59; V 149]

ORDINARY ISSUE   [G p. 68; R & D 564–65]
Green cloth. 300 copies.

LARGE PAPER ISSUE   [G p. 68; R & D 563]
Vellum. 30 numbered copies printed on Japan vellum.

Notes: Published in March 1897. The cover design, frontispiece, and three illustrations were reprinted in *The Poems of Ernest Dowson,* checklist no. 146.

115A. EINEN AUGENBLICK PIERROT. Mit zeichnungen von Aubrey Beardsley. München: Hyperion-Verlag, 1921.
By Beardsley: Front cover design, Smithers's "Puck on Pegasus" device, on title-page, frontispiece, initial letter, vignette, and cul-de-lampe (tailpiece) from first edition, checklist no. 115.
Vellum.   [G pp. 68–69]
Notes: 800 numbered copies. Translation (by Johannes von Guenther).

116. **Honoré de Balzac**
LA COMÉDIE HUMAINE OF HONORÉ DE BALZAC. "Scenes of Parisian life." Now for the first time completely translated into English. London: Leonard Smithers, 1897.
By Beardsley: Front cover ("Portrait of Balzac"), back cover (publisher's "Puck on Pegasus" device), and spine ("Mask") designs common to all 11 vols.
                                    [G 947–48; R 480–81; R & D 550, 552]

ORDINARY ISSUE   [R & D 562]
Scarlet cloth. 250 copies for sale in England.

SPECIAL ISSUE
Cream boards. 50 copies with the illustrations in two states.

Notes: The set contains 86 etchings by various French artists.

116A. LA COMÉDIE HUMAINE OF HONORÉ DE BALZAC. "Scenes of private life." London: Leonard Smithers, 1897–98.
By Beardsley: Cover designs retained from first series, checklist no. 116.
11 vols. Scarlet cloth.

117. **Jean Léonard**
THE SOUVENIRS OF LÉONARD. Hairdresser to Queen Marie-Antoinette. Now first rendered into English with a preface and annotations by A[lexander]. Teixeira de Mattos.[130] With two portraits. London: Privately printed [Leonard Smithers], 1897.
By Beardsley: Front cover design.
Two vols. Violet cloth. [G 1055; R 486; R & D 577; V 151]
Notes: Published in August 1897. 250 numbered copies with manuscript limitation statement on verso of half-title.

118. Bookplate for Olive Custance.[131] [September 1897].[132]
Legend reads "EX LIBRIS OLIVE CVSTANCE."
Photogravure. [G 1061; R 493; R & D 572–73; V 162; W 12]

119. **Gaston Vuillier**
A HISTORY OF DANCING FROM THE EARLIEST AGES TO OUR OWN TIMES. From the French of Gaston Vuillier. With a sketch of dancing in England by Joseph Grego. 23 full-page plates and 409 illustrations. London: William Heinemann, 1898.
By Beardsley: In special issue only: "Arbuscula" (photogravure printed in green), reproduced in Vol. 1 and also as plate in separate portfolio. Reprinted in *Under the Hill and Other Essays in Prose and Verse,* checklist no. 141.
Two vols. Dark brown cloth-backed pale green boards, with accompanying matching portfolio. [G 1062; R 494; R & D 571; V 163]
Notes: Published in November 1897 with postdated title-page. 35 numbered copies printed on Japan vellum signed by the publisher.

120. **Vincent O'Sullivan**
THE HOUSES OF SIN. London: Leonard Smithers, 1897.
By Beardsley: Design for front and back covers.
Imitation parchment. [G 1059; R 485; R & D 569; V 160]
Notes: Published ca. 26 October 1897. 400 numbered copies printed on Van Gelder paper. On 3 October 1897 Beardsley told Smithers, "O'Sullivan wants the design to be printed on both sides of the book," apparently following Wilde's dictum that "Nothing looks more vulgar and cheap than a book with an ornament on one side of the cover and the other side blank."[133]

---

[130] (1865–1921), translator and journalist, who married Lily Wilde, the widow of Oscar's brother William, in 1900.
[131] (1874–1944), poet, contributor to *The Yellow Book,* author of *Opals* (her first book of verse, published by John Lane in 1897) and other volumes of poetry. She eloped with Lord Alfred Douglas in 1902.
[132] *Letters* pp. 371–74.
[133] *Letters* p. 377 and note 1.

121. **Aubrey Beardsley**
SIX DRAWINGS ILLUSTRATING THÉOPHILE GAU-
TIER'S ROMANCE MADEMOISELLE DE MAUPIN. Lon-
don: Leonard Smithers, 1898.
By Beardsley: Six illustrations, the last of which, "The Lady with the Mon-
key," was intended as an illustration for *Volpone.*
Loose mounted photogravure plates, with separate title-page (colophon on
verso) and contents leaves, in blue-green cloth-backed grey-green board
portfolio.   [G 1084–89 and p. 69; R 487–92; R & D 574–76; V 164]
Notes: 50 numbered copies. Reproductions printed by Boussod, Valadon, and
Company. Beardsley intended to illustrate the entire book, to be published in
French in eight monthly parts; the project proved too demanding and expen-
sive and was abandoned in early November 1897.[134]

121A. "Mademoiselle de Maupin."
Gallatin states: "Mademoiselle de Maupin…was also printed in editions of
ten copies on white satin and fifteen on Japanese vellum, in color." Reade
confirms these figures, found in Smithers's October 1899 catalogue, which
also speaks of "4 Proofs on pure Vellum" priced at £5. 5s. each and "100 Lettered Prints on Plain Paper" priced at £1. 1s.   [G p. 69; R 487]

122. "The Identical." [London: Frederick H. Evans, May 1898].[135]
Platinotype by Evans of sketch of Shagpat (illustration for George
Meredith's 1856 novel, *The Shaving of Shagpat*) drawn in a letter to Evans
[May 1893]. Mounted on grey card and issued with facsimile of letter in grey
paper folder. The letter is reproduced in *Some Unknown Drawings of Aubrey
Beardsley,* checklist no. 170; the text printed in *Letters.*   [G 977; V 134]

123. THE IDLER. Vol. XIII, May 1898.
By Beardsley: 13 drawings, in article, "Aubrey Beardsley" by Max Beerbohm;
"The Return of Tannhäuser to the Venusberg"[136] appears for the first time.
Wrappers.   [G 863; R 391; R & D 439; V 103]

124. THE MAGAZINE OF ART. May 1898.
By Beardsley: Six drawings in article, "The Invention of Aubrey Beardsley" by
Aymer Vallance, five previously unpublished: "Perseus and the Monstre,"
"Sandro Botticelli," "Decorative Sketch Design of a Sailing Ship," "The Pro-
cession of Jeanne d'Arc" (pencil version), and "Angel Playing Hand-Organ."
Wrappers.   [G 196, 200, 239–40, 242; V 32–33, 47, 53–54]

---

[134] *Letters* pp. 354–55, 381–82, 384–85.
[135] So dated by Maggs Bros. in cat. 1108, *Books of the Nineties* (1990), item 20.
[136] The drawing is printed in reverse in both *The Idler* and *A Second Book of Fifty Drawings.* It is
reproduced properly in Reade Pl. 390.

125. THE STUDIO. Vol. XIII, No. 62, 14 May 1898.
By Beardsley: Six drawings in article, "Aubrey Beardsley in Memoriam" by G[leeson]. W[hite]., four published for the first time: "Chopin Ballade III. Op. 47," "Hail Mary," "Woman Reclining by a Meadow" (variant of drawing for Smithers's catalogue of rare books, checklist no. 90), and "Venus" (design intended for title-page of *The Story of Venus and Tannhäuser*).
Green wrappers.   [G 215, 865, 969; R 22, 320, 388; R & D 125, 442; V 18, 104, 120, 122]

126. THE POSTER. An illustrated monthly chronicle. Vol. 1, No. 3, August-September 1898.
By Beardsley: Three drawings in article, "Aubrey Beardsley at School" by Charles B. Cochran, one of which, "Holywell Street, London" (drawn ca. 1888), is published for the first time. The other two first appeared in the program and book of words for "The Pay of the Pied Piper," checklist no. 5.
Cream wrappers.   [G 137; R 13; V 11]

127. THE POSTER. An illustrated monthly chronicle. Vol. 1, No. 4, October 1898.
By Beardsley: Design for poster to advertise Singer sewing machines.
Cream wrappers.   [G 793; R 321; V 96]
Notes: Possibly commissioned in March 1894 (if the dating of a note to Lane, *Letters* p. 65, is correct), this poster—described as "unpublished" in the magazine—may have been printed in color by the Polychrome Printing Company, London, whose name appears in the lower left corner. No examples are listed in the major Beardsley exhibitions, and Gallatin refers only to the design's later reproduction in *A Second Book of Fifty Drawings*, checklist no. 132.

128. THE INTERNATIONAL SOCIETY OF SCULPTORS, PAINTERS, AND GRAVERS: ILLUSTRATED SOUVENIR CATALOGUE OF THE EXHIBITION OF INTERNATIONAL ART, KNIGHTSBRIDGE. Prepared by Carl Hentschel & Co. (Publishers to the Council). London: William Heinemann, 1898.
By Beardsley: "Messalina Returning Home."[137] Reprinted (without coloring) in *A Second Book of Fifty Drawings*, checklist no. 132.
Buff wrappers.   [G 951 and p. 123; R 393; R & D 473; V 126]
Notes: Published in November 1898 (exhibition took place in May). The catalogue lists 23 drawings by Beardsley, along with designs for book covers.

---

[137] So titled by Reade, R & D, and the owner, the Tate Gallery, this drawing was called "Messalina Returning from the Bath" in the International Society's *Catalogue* (and by Gallatin), and "Messalina" in *A Second Book of Fifty Drawings*.

129. **Ben Jonson**

BEN JONSON HIS VOLPONE. Or the foxe. A new edition. With a critical essay on the author by Vincent O'Sullivan and a frontispiece, five initial letters, and a cover design illustrative and decorative by Aubrey Beardsley. Together with an eulogy of the artist by Robert Ross. London: Leonard Smithers, 1898.

By Beardsley: Front cover design (also on first preliminary leaf), back cover design (publisher's "Puck on Pegasus" device, also on title-page), frontispiece, and five initial letters. [G 1090–96; R 495–502; R & D 581–82, 584; V 165]

ORDINARY ISSUE   [G p. 69; R & D 579]

Blue-green cloth. 1,000 numbered copies printed on art paper.

Notes: Unnumbered copies are frequently encountered, lending credence to the belief that more than the 1,000 stated were printed.

SPECIAL ISSUE   [G pp. 69–70; R & D 580, 583]

By Beardsley: Additional reproductions of initial letters printed (photogravure plates) in large size.

Vellum. 100 numbered copies printed on Japan vellum.[138]

Notes: Published in mid-December 1898. Copies of both issues with the imprint of John Lane, New York replacing that of Smithers on title-page and foot of spine (retaining Smithers's "Puck on Pegasus" device on title-page) formed American sub-issues. Gallatin also notes: "Some copies with Smithers' imprint have The Bodley Head printed on the spine." Beardsley began *Volpone,* his last major work, in November 1897. What was envisioned as an *édition de luxe*—with 24 illustrations, frontispiece, initial letters, and small drawings—appeared with only the frontispiece, five initials, and front cover design completed by the time of the artist's death on 16 March 1898. The text was anonymously edited by Ernest Dowson.[139] Ross's eulogy formed the basis for his 1909 book, *Aubrey Beardsley,* checklist no. 154.[140]

129A. Prospectus for *Volpone.* [July 1898].[141]

By Beardsley: Frontispiece reproduced on first page. Text incorporates notes written by Beardsley in December 1897, a draft of which was printed—and manuscript reproduced—in *A Beardsley Miscellany,* checklist no. 190.[142]

Folded leaf.   [G p. 70]

---

[138] The leaves are slightly larger due to the untrimmed fore and bottom edges, top edge gilt.

[139] *The Letters of Ernest Dowson,* pp. 402–3.

[140] Ross presented copies of *Volpone* in December 1898 to Max Beerbohm and Joseph Pennell using the inscription "With Ben Jonson's compliments."

[141] Dated from postmark (25 July 1898) on a copy sent to Joseph Pennell, found inserted in a copy of the book in the Rare Book and Special Collections Division, Library of Congress.

[142] See also *Letters* pp. 403–4.

129B. VOLPONE VON BEN JONSON. Mit initalen, einem titelblatt und deckel von Aubrey Beardsley. Autorisierte deutsche ausgabe von Margarete Mauthner. Berlin: Bruno Cassirer, 1910.
By Beardsley: Front cover design, frontispiece, and five initial letters from first edition, checklist no. 129.

ORDINARY ISSUE   [G p. 70]
Purple cloth. Nos. 51–650 of 650 numbered copies printed on laid paper.

SPECIAL ISSUE   [G p. 70]
Vellum. Nos. 1–50 of 650 numbered copies printed on Van Gelder paper.

Notes: Imitation of first edition (including Smithers's "Puck on Pegasus" device on title-page). Initial letters also printed enlarged on Japan vellum plates.

129C. BEN JONSON'S VOLPONE. Eine lieblose komodie in drei akten von Ben Jonson, frei bearbeitet, von Stefan Zweig, mit sechs bildern nach Aubrey Beardsley. Potsdam: Gustav Kiepenheuer Verlag, 1927 [or 1926?].

129D. BEN JONSON'S VOLPONE. A loveless comedy in 3 acts. Freely adapted by Stefan Zweig and translated from the German by Ruth Langner. New York: Viking Press, 1928.
By Beardsley: Frontispiece, initial letter (on title-page, also on dust jacket), and cover design (also on endpapers) from first edition, checklist no. 129. Tan cloth, dust jacket.

130. **Arthur Symons**
AUBREY BEARDSLEY. London: At the Sign of the Unicorn, 1898.
By Beardsley: Six drawings, two of which, "Le Débris d'un Poète" and "The Mirror of Love"[143] are published for the first time.
White cloth-backed grey boards.   [G 208, 1051, and p. 79; R 31, 386; R & D 127, 555; V 41, 142]
Notes: Published in December 1898. Based on article in *The Fortnightly Review,* May 1898. Reset edition with 16 drawings published by Unicorn Press, London, in 1948, and by John Baker, London, in 1966, 1967, and 1971.

130A. [SECOND EDITION]. New edition, revised & enlarged. London: J. M. Dent, 1905.
By Beardsley: 29 drawings, of which two, "Raphael Sanzio" and an unused binding design for the Bon-Mots Series, are published for the first time, along with a facsimile of the manuscript of Beardsley's version of Catullus's "Carmen CI."   [G 244, 772, and p. 79; R 30; R & D 129; V 48, 66]

---

[143] Intended as frontispiece to André Raffalovich's verse volume, *The Thread and the Path* (1895), but rejected by the publisher, David Nutt, because of the nude figure; see *Letters* pp. 86–89.

ORDINARY ISSUE
Green cloth-backed green boards.

LARGE PAPER ISSUE [G 856–57 and p. 79; R 36]
By Beardsley: Two additional, previously unpublished drawings (intended illustrations for *Evelina*), not included in ordinary copies.
Vellum-backed green boards. 150 numbered copies.

Notes: Published in December 1905. Enlarged by the inclusion of text by Symons published in *The Saturday Review*. A French edition, translated by Jack Cohen and Edouard and Louis Thomas, was issued by Floury, Paris in 1906.

130B. THE ART OF AUBREY BEARDSLEY. Introduction by Arthur Symons. New York: Boni and Liveright, [1918].
By Beardsley: 63 reproductions.
Brown cloth (also dark green cloth). [G p. 79]
Notes: Vol. XLII of the Modern Library of the World's Best Books. Published in early 1918. The text is from the 1905 edition of *Aubrey Beardsley*, checklist no. 130A. Reprinted by the Modern Library, New York, ca. 1925–35.[144]

131. "Sir Edward Burne-Jones." [1899].
Process reproduction of pen-and-ink and wash portrait by Beardsley dated 12 July 1891.[145] Issued in an edition of eight numbered copies by the London bookseller James Tregaskis in 1899. The drawing was reprinted in *The Critic* (New York), December 1902, checklist no. 137.
India paper. [G 183; V 22]

132. **Aubrey Beardsley**
A SECOND BOOK OF FIFTY DRAWINGS. London: Leonard Smithers, 1899.
By Beardsley: 50 drawings, of which 29 are published for the first time, front cover design (adapted from "A Footnote," self-portrait first published in No. 2 of *The Savoy*), and back cover design (publisher's "Puck on Pegasus" device, repeated on title-page). [R 428]

ORDINARY ISSUE [G p. 73; R & D 568]
Red cloth. 1,000 copies printed on art paper.

LARGE PAPER ISSUE [G p. 73]
Vellum. 50 numbered copies printed on Japan vellum.

---

[144] George M. Andes, *A Descriptive Bibliography of The Modern Library, 1917–1970* (1989), pp. 21–22, describes the first edition and one later impression. Like virtually all Modern Library titles, *The Art of Aubrey Beardsley* was reprinted at different times and in different bindings.
[145] *Letters* p. 29. Gallatin gives the date incorrectly as 12 June.

Notes: Published in February 1899. Contains a preface by Smithers dated 19 December 1898.[146] American issue copies have "New York John Lane 140 Fifth Avenue 1899" on title-page and "John Lane 1899" at foot of spine.

133. **Aubrey Beardsley**
THE EARLY WORK OF AUBREY BEARDSLEY. With a prefatory note by H. C. Marillier. London: John Lane, 1899.
By Beardsley: 179 drawings, 21 published for the first time.[147] Also front cover design (adapted from frontispiece and title-page designs for *The Story of Venus and Tannhäuser*), spine ornament (from spines of Vols. III–V of *The Yellow Book*), and title-page design—all used in subsequent editions and also for *The Later Work,* checklist no. 136, and for *The Uncollected Work,* checklist no. 177. Back cover stamped with Beardsley's three-candle device.   [R 37, 390]
ORDINARY ISSUE   [G p. 74]
Cream cloth stamped in green.

SPECIAL ISSUE   [G p. 74]
Cream cloth stamped in gilt. 120 copies (100 for sale) printed on Japan vellum.

Notes: Published 2 March 1899.

133A. [SECOND EDITION]. London: John Lane, 1912.
By Beardsley: 179 drawings, plus reproduction of cover of *Le Morte Darthur.*
Blue-green cloth.   [G p. 74]
Notes: Published in October 1911 with postdated title-page. Publisher's note states that "there has been considerable rearrangement of the plates. Many that originally appeared in the Later Work are now transferred to this volume, and conversely, in order to preserve a proper chronological sequence."

133B. [THIRD EDITION]. London: John Lane, 1920.
By Beardsley: 179 drawings, plus reproduction of cover of *Le Morte Darthur.*
Blue cloth, dust jacket.   [G p. 74]
Notes: Published in May? 1920. Reprints (somewhat altered) were issued in 1967 by Dover Publications, and by Da Capo Press, both New York.

134. **A[lbert]. E[ugene]. Gallatin**
LIST OF DRAWINGS BY AUBREY BEARDSLEY. New York: M. F. Mansfield and A. Wessels, 1900.
Grey boards, printed label on front cover.   [G p. 76]

---

[146] Smithers announced *A Third Book of Fifty Drawings* in his October 1899 catalogue, but the volume never appeared.
[147] Japan vellum "proofs" were printed for some of the illustrations (Warrack and Perkins 96).

Notes: 100 copies. Printed by the De Vinne Press, New York, in December 1899. A bibliography listing items published 1895–1900, intended to supplement Vallance's iconography in *A Book of Fifty Drawings*, checklist no. 112.

135. PAST AND PRESENT. The magazine of the Brighton Grammar School. E. J. Marshall Memorial Number, December 1900.
By Beardsley: Four illustrations to "Traveling in the U.S.A. and Canada," lantern slide drawings made (Fall 1888) to accompany lecture by E. J. Marshall. Also reprints one drawing from "The Pay of the Pied Piper," checklist no. 5.
Blue cloth. [G 138–41 and p. 21]

135A. ["Traveling in the U.S.A. and Canada."]
Separate printing of the illustrations from *Past and Present*, checklist no. 135.
Loose plates. [G p. 21]
Notes: Gallatin states that "a few sets" of the illustrations "were printed on plate paper." The date given, "(1891)," is surely incorrect.

136. **Aubrey Beardsley**
THE LATER WORK OF AUBREY BEARDSLEY. London: John Lane, 1901.
By Beardsley: 173 drawings, including 16 complete and two partial drawings published for the first time, plus reproduction of cover of *Le Morte Darthur*.

ORDINARY ISSUE [G pp. 74–75]
Cream cloth stamped in red.

SPECIAL ISSUE [G pp. 74–75]
Cream cloth stamped in gilt. 120 copies printed on Japan vellum, with frontispiece, "Mademoiselle de Maupin," hand-colored, and the initial letters for *Volpone* are reproduced (original size) in photogravure, not half-tone.[148]

Notes: Published 7 November 1900 with postdated title-page. Prefaced by an unsigned publisher's note by John Lane. Front cover design, spine ornament, and title-page design are from *The Early Work*, checklist no. 133.

136A. [SECOND EDITION]. London: John Lane, 1912.
By Beardsley: 173 drawings.
Pale blue cloth. [G p. 75]
Notes: Published in October 1911 with postdated title-page. Illustrations rearranged and redistributed in conjunction with changes made in the 1912 edition of *The Early Work*, checklist no. 133A.

---

[148] As advertised by Lane. Possibly 100 or 125 were printed, some copies bearing a manuscript number on recto of frontispiece; see Colbeck, Vol. 1, p. 42. One or more photogravure plates may be found in ordinary copies; the placement in the two issues was apparently irregular.

136B. [THIRD EDITION]. London: John Lane, 1920.
By Beardsley: 173 drawings.
Blue cloth.   [G p. 75]
Notes: Published in March 1920. Plate numbers added in this edition.

136C. [FOURTH EDITION]. London: John Lane, [1930].
By Beardsley: 173 drawings.
Blue cloth, dust jacket.
Notes: Minor changes were made. Reprints with slight alterations were issued in 1967 by Dover Publications, and Da Capo Press, both New York.

137. THE CRITIC. New York, Vol. XLI, December 1902.
By Beardsley: Eight drawings in article, "Notes on the Literary Element in Beardsley's Art" by A. E. Gallatin, of which one, "Katharina Klavsky, as Isolde," is published for the first time. Another, "Sir Edward Burne-Jones," checklist no. 131, had been privately printed in 1898.
White wrappers.   [G 982 and p. 84; R 28; R & D 130; V 118]

138. A[lbert]. E[ugene]. Gallatin
AUBREY BEARDSLEY AS A DESIGNER OF BOOK-PLATES. London: Elkin Mathews, 1902.
By Beardsley: Bookplates for John Lumsden Propert and Olive Custance, checklist nos. 51 and 118.

ORDINARY ISSUE   [G pp. 76–77]
Pale blue-grey boards. 85 copies printed on handmade paper.

SPECIAL ISSUE   [G pp. 76–77]
Japan vellum. Three copies printed on Japan vellum.

Notes: Published in December 1902.[149] Printed by the De Vinne Press and co-published by Charles E. Peabody, Boston. Back cover reproduces Beardsley's three-candle device. Gallatin's essay and the two illustrations also appeared in *The Reader* (New York), December 1902 [G p. 84].

139. Aubrey Beardsley
DRAWINGS FOR THE SIXTH SATIRE OF JUVENAL. London: Jesus Press, 1903.
By Beardsley: Three previously unpublished illustrations to Juvenal.[150]
Loose plates.   [R 468–70; R & D 468–70]
Notes: Probably issued by Smithers, possibly with a fictitious date. In 1906 the illustrations were reprinted (or the plates themselves reused) in *An Issue of Five Drawings Illustrative of Juvenal and Lucian*, checklist no. 149.

---

[149] Nelson, *Elkin Mathews*, p. 213, no. 1902.17 in his checklist of Mathews publications.
[150] Beardsley's plan to also translate the Sixth Satire never materialized (*Letters* p. 149, note 3).

140. **A[lbert]. E[ugene]. Gallatin**
AUBREY BEARDSLEY'S DRAWINGS. A catalogue and a list of
criticisms. New York: Godfrey A. S. Wieners, 1903.
By Beardsley: Six drawings, of which one, "Max Alvary" (in the role of
Tristan), is published for the first time. Reprinted in *The Uncollected Work,*
checklist no. 177. [G 981 and p. 77; R 32; R & D 132; V 117]

ORDINARY ISSUE
Parchment-backed dark grey boards. 220 numbered copies.

SPECIAL ISSUE
Parchment. 30 numbered copies interleaved with blank writing paper.

Notes: Published 2 May 1903. 250 copies printed in all.[151] Printed by J. J. Little, New York, and co-published by Elkin Mathews, London. Back cover reproduces Beardsley's three-candle device. There is "An Addendum" leaflet
(1904) of four pages listing more items.

141. **Aubrey Beardsley**
UNDER THE HILL AND OTHER ESSAYS IN PROSE AND
VERSE. With illustrations. London: John Lane, 1904.
By Beardsley: 17 drawings, three of which, "Fred Brown, N. E. A. C.," a
sketch of seven heads, and "L'Abbé Mouret" (intended frontispiece to Emile
Zola's novel, *La Faute de l'Abbé Mouret*) are published for the first time. Front
cover design adapted from original cover design for *Salome.* Contains most
of Beardsley's writings: "Under the Hill" (expurgated version of *The Story of
Venus and Tannhäuser*),[152] "The Three Musicians," "The Ballad of a Barber,"
and translation of Catullus's "Carmen ci," all from *The Savoy,* checklist no.
103, along with two letters to the press, checklist nos. 68 and 61, and "Table
Talk of Aubrey Beardsley."[153]   [G 194, 205–6, and pp. 106–7; R & D 126]

ORDINARY ISSUE   [R & D 447]
Blue-green cloth.[154]

SPECIAL ISSUE
Cream cloth. 50 copies printed on Japan vellum.[155]

---

[151] Nelson, *Elkin Mathews,* p. 213, no. 1903.8 in his checklist of Mathews publications.
[152] The title "Under the Hill" may have been derived from Under-the-Hill, the Gloucestershire
home of More Adey's family; see John Adlard, *Stenbock, Yeats, and the Nineties* (1969), p. 52.
[153] *Letters* p. 139, note 2. The "Table Talk" was "a projected small volume of aphorisms and illustrations" which Beardsley worked on in the summer of 1896.
[154] According to Frank Hollings cat. 170 (1931), item 39, "later issues were in green" cloth. Copies in blue cloth with "THE BODLEY HEAD" in place of "JOHN LANE" on the spine are known.
[155] The book contains no limitation statement. Documentation of the number of copies printed
is found in a letter from Lane to R. A. Walker, 26 October 1915, inserted in a special issue copy
of the book in the Rare Book and Special Collections Division, Library of Congress.

Notes: Published 2 October 1903 with postdated title-page. The publisher's note contains much the same text as John Lane's other writings on Beardsley. Reprinted by Lane in 1913 and 1921, and (with plain front cover) again in 1928 and in 1930, all bound in green cloth. A paperback facsimile of the first edition, with an introduction by Edward Lucie-Smith, "Aubrey Beardsley and *Under the Hill*," was published by Paddington Press, New York, in 1977.

141A. UNTER DEM HUGEL. Eine romantische novelle von Aubrey Beardsley. Leipzig: Insel-Verlag, 1905.
By Beardsley: Frontispiece, "Ave Atque Vale."
Olive suede, stamped label on front cover.
Notes: 500 numbered copies. Translations (by Rudolf A. Schröder) of "Under the Hill," "The Three Musicians," "The Ballad of a Barber," and Catullus's "Carmen CI." Reprinted in 1909. The "Under the Hill" translation, with five illustrations, was reprinted by Insel-Verlag, Frankfurt, in 1965.

141B. SOUS LA COLLINE. Paris: H. Floury, 1908.
By Beardsley: 13 drawings.

ORDINARY ISSUE   [G pp. 108–9]
Grey boards. 975 copies printed on imitation vellum.

SPECIAL ISSUE   [G pp. 108–9]
25 copies printed on Van Gelder paper.

Notes: Printed in October 1907. Translations (by Arthur Jacob Hendrik Cornette) of "Under the Hill," "The Three Musicians," "The Ballad of a Barber," Catullus's "Carmen CI," and "Table Talk of Aubrey Beardsley." Preface by Jacques-Emile Blanche.

141C. UNDER THE HILL. Girard, Kans.: Haldeman-Julius, [ca. 1931].
Blue wrappers.
Notes: Little Blue Books Series No. 1643. Text of "Under the Hill" only.

142. [John Lane]
AUBREY BEARDSLEY & THE YELLOW BOOK. London: John Lane, 1903.
By Beardsley: Eight drawings, and texts of two letters to the press previously reprinted in *Under the Hill and Other Essays,* checklist no. 141.
Grey wrappers.   [G p. 86]
Notes: Promotes Beardsley-illustrated works available from Lane; some titles from the 1890s were still for sale in 1903 at advanced prices. Front cover design adapted from cover of *A Book of Fifty Drawings,* checklist no. 112. A German edition (English text) with Berlin imprint has prices in marks.

143. DRAWINGS BY AUBREY BEARDSLEY. [London:] Carfax &
Co., [October 1904].
Red wrappers.   [G p. 123]
Notes: The first comprehensive Beardsley exhibition, listing 100 drawings.

144. **Aubrey Beardsley**
LAST LETTERS OF AUBREY BEARDSLEY. With an introduc-
tory note by the Rev. John Gray. London: Longmans, Green, 1904.
By Beardsley: 162 letters (plus four telegrams) to André Raffalovich, with 14
other letters (three to John Gray).
Grey cloth, dust jacket.   [G pp. 115–17; R & D 595]
Notes: Published in December 1904. Includes an account of the artist's fu-
neral, possibly written by Mabel Beardsley (p. 155). A facsimile was pub-
lished by Folcroft Library Editions, Folcroft, Pa., in 1973. Insel-Verlag,
Leipzig, issued a German translation, *Aubrey Beardsleys letzte Briefe,* in 1910.

145. **A[lbert]. E[ugene]. G[allatin].**
WHISTLER'S ART DICTA AND OTHER ESSAYS. Boston:
Charles E. Goodspeed, 1904.
By Beardsley: Unfinished border design for *Le Morte Darthur* [G 629], fac-
simile (folding plate) of illustrated letter to Smithers, 8 December [1897],
and sketch from a letter, in "Notes on Three Hitherto Unpublished Draw-
ings by Beardsley." Another letter to Smithers, 26 December [1897], and
Catullus's "Carmen ci" are printed in "Aubrey Beardsley: Man of Letters."
Blue cloth-backed marbled boards, printed label on spine.   [G pp. 84–85]
Notes: Published in December 1904. 175 copies.[156] Printed by the Merry-
mount Press, Boston, and co-published by Elkin Mathews, London.

146. **Ernest Dowson**
THE POEMS OF ERNEST DOWSON. With a memoir by Arthur
Symons. Four illustrations by Aubrey Beardsley, and a portrait by William
Rothenstein. London: John Lane, 1905.
By Beardsley: Five designs (initial letter, front cover,[157] frontispiece, vignette,
and cul-de-lampe) from *The Pierrot of the Minute,* checklist no. 117. Front
cover design (repeated on dust jacket) from cover of *Verses,* checklist no. 106.
Green cloth, red-orange dust jacket.
Notes: Published in May 1905. Reprints (some with American issues) were
published by Lane in 1906, 1909, 1911, 1913, 1915, 1917, etc.

---

[156] Nelson, *Elkin Mathews,* p. 216, no. 1904.20 in his checklist of Mathews publications.
[157] Described incorrectly as "half-title" in list of illustrations, p. xxxv.

147. "Head of an Angel." [December 1905].
"Printed in 4-inch square form on card for private distribution, Christmas 1905." Presumably issued by Mabel Beardsley, the then owner.[158] The drawing (ca. 1892) had appeared in *A Second Book of Fifty Drawings*, checklist no. 132, and in *The Later Work*, checklist no. 136.   [G 210; V 43]

148. "Head of a Chinese Priest" and "Head of a Satyr." [London: Leonard Smithers, ca. 1906].
Two grotesques from the Bon-Mots Series, reproduced in an edition of "25 copies only printed on folio sheet, and 10 copies only in red."[159] Vallance attributes this to James Tregaskis, the London antiquarian bookseller. The issuer was Smithers—or, possibly, there were multiple versions. Two copies at Princeton are numbered, inscribed, and signed by Smithers; another, "numbered and inscribed by Leonard Smithers on verso," was described in a Maggs Bros. catalogue,[160] where a connection is made to the drawings' appearance in the publisher's edition of Wilde's *Phrases and Philosophies of the Young* (1906, dated 1903).[161]
Line block on Japan vellum.   [R 240; V 99]

149. **Aubrey Beardsley**
AN ISSUE OF FIVE DRAWINGS ILLUSTRATIVE OF JUVENAL AND LUCIAN. London: [Leonard Smithers], 1906.
By Beardsley: Five drawings, three illustrating Juvenal's "Sixth Satire," and two prepared for *Lucian's True History*, checklist no. 78, but not used. All reprinted in the special issue of *The Uncollected Work*, checklist no. 177.
Loose plates printed on Japan vellum, with title-page, list of illustrations, and colophon leaves printed on paper, in reddish-plum paper portfolio.[162]
[G 1074–78 and pp. 67–68; R 257–58, 468–70;
R & D 298, 468–70; V 74 III–IV]
Notes: 120 numbered copies. Reade and Dickinson variously date this to 1897 and 1899 as well as 1905, the year given by Gallatin. The prospectus (printed on paper) includes the introductory material from the colophon leaf.

149A. FOUR DESIGNS FOR THE "SIXTH SATIRE" OF JUVENAL AND TWO UNPUBLISHED DESIGNS FOR "LUCIAN'S TRUE HISTORY." London: Private print [*sic*], 1915.

---

[158] "A Christmas Carol," V 45, would seem also to have been used by Mabel Beardsley for a Christmas card, "in photogravure, 3 inches diameter, for private circulation."
[159] Vallance 99.
[160] Maggs Bros. cat. 1108, *Books of the Nineties* (1990), item 32.
[161] Mason 603–4.
[162] The title-page and list of illustrations are lacking in some copies.

By Beardsley: Six drawings: five from *An Issue of Five Drawings Illustrative of Juvenal and Lucian,* checklist no. 149, plus "Messalina Returning from the Bath" [R 483].
Loose plates (watermarked "Alexandra Japan") in blue wrappers.
Notes: This edition was apparently unrecorded until described by Warrack and Perkins: "This is probably a Nichols piracy. It follows closely Smithers' 1906 edition…in exactly the same size, though with a coarsening of both line and dot work."[163]

150. EXPOSITION DES DESSINS D'AUBREY BEARDSLEY, 1872–1898. Paris: Galeries Shirleys, February 1907.
Cream wrappers. [G p. 123]
Notes: Lists 93 drawings and posters. Front cover reproduces "Venus Between Terminal Gods." Prefatory note by Herbert Charles Pollitt and extract from Robert Ross's eulogy in *Volpone,* checklist no. 129.

151. **Aubrey Beardsley**
THE STORY OF VENUS AND TANNHÄUSER. In which is set forth an exact account of the manner of state held by Madame Venus, goddess and meretrix, under the famous Hörselberg, and containing the adventures of Tannhäuser in that place, his repentance, his journeying to Rome and return to the loving mountain. A romantic novel. Now first printed from the original manuscript. London: For private circulation [Leonard Smithers], 1907.
By Beardsley: The first "complete" text of the unfinished "Under the Hill" using its original title. An expurgated version had appeared in *The Savoy,* checklist no. 103, and in *Under the Hill and Other Essays,* checklist no. 141.

ORDINARY ISSUE [G pp. 107–8]
Gray boards, printed label on front cover. 250 numbered copies.

SPECIAL ISSUE [G pp. 107–8; R & D 443–44]
Vellum (also cloth). 50 numbered copies printed on Japan vellum.

Notes: Beardsley was working on the novel in late 1894 and Lane announced publication for early 1895.[164] After the first (expurgated) chapters appeared in *The Savoy,* "Smithers announced [in the July 1896 issue] that serialization was discontinued, but that it would be published in book form with numerous illustrations as soon as Beardsley was well enough to complete it."[165]

---

[163] Warrack and Perkins, *Short List Thirty-Three* (Spring 1986), item 3.
[164] *Letters* p. 76. The book, which was to contain 24 full-page illustrations, was advertised as "in preparation" in Lane's catalogue published in Vol. III of *The Yellow Book* (October 1894).
[165] *Letters* p. 135, note 1.

151A. DIE GESCHICHTE VON VENUS UND TANN-
HAUSER. Worein gewebt ist eine genaue beschreibung der sitten am hof-
staate der Frau Venus, göttin und buhlerin in dem berüchtigten Hörselberge,
woran die abenteuer Tannhäusers daselbst, seine reue, seine fahrt nach Rom
und seine rückkehr zum liebesberg geschlossen sind. Eine romantische novelle. Erste übersetzung nach dem originaldruck des manuskriptes. [Mu-
nich: Hans von Weber, 1909].
Vellum.   [G p. 109]
Notes: 246 numbered copies. Front cover and colophon reproduce Beardsley's three-candle device.

151B. [ANOTHER EDITION]. In die verwebt ist eine ausführliche
schilderung der sitten am hofe der Frau Venus, göttin und buhlerin, in dem
berüchtigten Hörselberge, und an die sich anschliessen die abenteuer Tannhäusers daselbst. [Munich, 1920].
By Beardsley: Seven drawings.
Yellow marbled boards, printed label on front cover.
Notes: 350 numbered copies. Translation (by Curt Moreck).

151C. VENUS UND TANNHAUSER. Eine romantische novelle.
Hannover: Paul Steegemann Verlag, [1920].
Parchment-backed red boards.
Notes: 1,100 numbered copies. Translation (by Prokop Templin). Chapters
one to ten by Beardsley; 11 to 18 and epilogue by Franz Blei.

151D. DAS HAUS DER TAUSEND FREUDEN. Fragment. Berlin:
Eigenbrödlerverlag, [1920].
Buff wrappers.
Notes: 600 numbered copies. Translation.

151E. VENUS AND TANNHAUSER. Privatly [*sic*] printed, [ca.
1920?].
Red cloth.
Notes: 500 numbered copies. No indication of place or date of printing, but
likely issued during the 1920s. The author is referred to as "Audrey Beardsley" on front cover and title-page.

151F. THE STORY OF VENUS AND TANNHÄUSER.... A ro-
mantic novel. New York: Issued privately for subscribers only. 1927.
Gold silk-backed black boards in slipcase.   [G p. 108]
Notes: 750 numbered copies. Issued by N. L. Brown. Text of first edition,
checklist no. 151, with 16 drawings by Bertram R. Elliott.

151G. EROTISCHE NOVELLE. Mit neun zeichnungen. Privatdruck, [1930].
By Beardsley: Nine drawings.
Peach cloth.

ORDINARY ISSUE
Nos. 51–300 of 300 numbered copies (some numbered higher than 300).

SPECIAL ISSUE
Nos. 1–50 of 300 numbered copies printed on handmade paper.

151H. UNDER THE HILL. The story of Venus and Tannhäuser, in which is set forth an exact account of the manner of state held by Madam Venus, goddess & meretrix, under the famous Horselberg, and containing the adventures of Tannhäuser in that place, his journeying to Rome and return to the loving mountain. Now completed by John Glassco. Paris: The Olympia Press, 1959.
By Beardsley: Frontispiece and title-page designs for *The Story of Venus and Tannhäuser,* six drawings from *The Savoy,* and two related works, "Venus between Terminal Gods" and "Venus" (design intended for title-page of *The Story of Venus and Tannhäuser*).
Green cloth in slipcase.
Notes: 3,000 numbered copies. Text from the 1927 edition, checklist no. 151F, "completed" by Glassco. Reprinted by the New English Library, London, in 1966 (No. 105 in The Olympia Press Traveler's Companion Series). Another edition was published by Grove Press, New York, in 1959, and reprinted in 1967. A Dutch translation was published by Uitgeverij De Arbeiderspers, Amsterdam, in 1971.

151I. L'HISTOIRE DE VENUS ET TANNHAUSER. Nouvelle romantique. Traduite par Odile Colonna. Paris: Le Terrain Vague, [1963].
By Beardsley: Six drawings.
Buff wrappers.

151J. BAJO EL MONTE. Traducción y prólogo Miguel Toledo. Buenos Aires: Arca/Galerna, [1967].
Notes: Portuguese translation.

151K. THE STORY OF VENUS AND TANNHÄUSER....A romantic novel. New York: Award Books, [1967].
By Beardsley: Frontispiece and title-page designs for *The Story of Venus and Tannhäuser,* plus 80 drawings, cover designs, etc. from *Le Morte Darthur, Salome, The Rape of the Lock,* the Keynotes Series, and other works.
Black wrappers.

Notes: Text of first edition, checklist no. 151, with introduction by Paul J. Gillette. Co-published by Tandem Books, London (copies for England have wrappers printed in the U.S. with price of five shillings on front cover). Front and back covers reproduce detail from "The Masque of the Red Death."

151L. DIE GESCHICHTE VON VENUS UND TANNHAUSER. ... Eine romantische novelle mit zeichnungen von Norbert Kaspar. Wiesbaden: Verlag Offizin Parvus, [1967].
Notes: 50 numbered copies signed by Kaspar.

151M. [ANOTHER EDITION]. Das berühmte erotische prosawerk des künstlers. Illustriert mit 73 seiner zeichnungen, ergänzt durch eine briefauswahl und erläutert in einem ausführlichen nachwort. Munich: Heyne, [1968].
By Beardsley: 73 drawings, cover designs, etc. from *Le Morte Darthur*, *Salome*, *The Rape of the Lock*, the Keynotes Series, and other works.
White wrappers.
Notes: Translation (by Jochen Wilkat), plus 28 letters to Smithers.

151N. THE STORY OF VENUS AND TANNHÄUSER. Or "Under the Hill."...A romantic novel. With twelve illustrations from the author's own hand and two illustrations from photographs. Edited with an introduction by Robert Oresko. London: Academy Editions, [1974].
By Beardsley: 13 drawings.
Black cloth, dust jacket (also pink wrappers).
Notes: Text based on first edition, checklist no. 151, with two passages in chapter VII interpolated from *The Savoy*, No. 2, April 1896. Front cover design (on dust jacket or front wrapper) adapted from cover and title-page for *Grey Roses*, checklist no. 34.

151O. [ANOTHER EDITION]. In which is set forth an exact account of the manner of state held by Madam Venus, goddess & meretrix, under the famous Horselberg, and containing the adventures of Tannhauser in that place, his journeying to Rome and return to the loving mountain. London: Bracken Books, [1985].
By Beardsley: Frontispiece and title-page designs for *The Story of Venus and Tannhäuser*, plus 46 drawings, cover designs, etc. from *Le Morte Darthur*, *Salome*, *The Rape of the Lock*, the Bon-Mots Series and Keynotes Series, and other works.
Black cloth, dust jacket.
Notes: Text of first edition, checklist no. 151. Also contains forgery, "Adoration of the Penis."

152. **Aubrey Beardsley**
BRIEFE. Kalendernotizen und die vier zeichnungen zu E. A. Poe. Von
Aubrey Beardsley. Munich: Hans von Weber, 1908.
By Beardsley: Four Poe illustrations, checklist no. 80, and 181 letters to
Smithers, translated by their then owner, Fritz Waerndorfer.

ORDINARY ISSUE   [G pp. 117–18]
Grey boards. Nos. 26–525 of 525 copies printed on handmade paper.

SPECIAL ISSUE   [G pp. 117–18]
Leather. Nos. 1–25 of 525 copies printed on Japan vellum.

Notes. Preface by Franz Blei. Includes some "notes" purportedly written by
Beardsley in a notebook. R. A. Walker condemned the work as "inaccurate
and badly edited…so full of errors and omissions as to be untrustworthy."[166]

153. CATALOGUE OF AN EXHIBITION OF DRAWINGS BY
AUBREY BEARDSLEY. [London:] The Baillie Gallery, August and
September 1909.
White wrappers.   [G p. 124]
Notes: Lists 118 drawings, several reproductions, and five letters to Smithers.

154. **Robert Ross**
AUBREY BEARDSLEY. With sixteen full-page illustrations and a revised iconography by Aymer Vallance. London: John Lane, 1909.
By Beardsley: 16 drawings.
Red cloth, orange dust jacket.   [G p. 78]
Notes: Published in December 1908 with postdated title-page. Text first appeared as the eulogy in *Volpone*, checklist no. 129. The iconography is a revised version of the one published in *A Book of Fifty Drawings*, checklist no.
112. Title-page adapted from *Keynotes*, checklist no. 25, and front cover (also
dust jacket) bears title-page and cover ornament from Davidson's *Plays*,
checklist no. 58. Lane published a second edition (in blue-grey cloth) in 1921.

155. **Martin Birnbaum**
AUBREY VINCENT BEARDSLEY. New York: Berlin Photo-
graphic Company, 1911.
Blue wrappers.   [G p. 124]
Notes: Essay by Birnbaum[167] followed by "Catalogue of the First American
Exhibition of the Original Work of Aubrey Beardsley" held at the Berlin

---

[166] *Letters from Aubrey Beardsley to Leonard Smithers*, checklist no. 184, p. xii.
[167] Reprinted in slightly different form in Birnbaum's *Introductions: Painters, Sculptors, and
Graphic Artists* (1919).

Photographic Company, New York, 21 October–10 November 1911. Lists
79 drawings, along with books and posters (described in "Bibliography" at
end). The exhibition subsequently moved to the Art Institute of Chicago (7–
25 December 1911) and to the Buffalo Fine Arts Academy/Albright Art
Gallery, Buffalo, New York (1–31 January 1912); variant versions of this publication were issued for each of these venues.[168]

156. [Reproductions of 12 drawings]. [London: Frederick H. Evans, 1913?].
Platinotypes by Evans of 12 grotesques for the Bon-Mots Series.
Loose plates in paper folder.   [G p. 38; R & D 281?]
Notes: 50 copies privately printed. According to Reade and Dickinson this or
a similar set was issued in 1919 in an edition of 250 copies. [169]

157. [Reproduction of self-portrait]. [London: Frederick H. Evans, 1913].
Platinotype by Evans of drawing made on back of envelope [ca. 1893].
Loose plate.   [G 241; V 133?]
Notes: 50 copies privately printed.

158. [Facsimile of letter to Leonard Smithers]. [London: R. A. Walker, July 1913].
Four-page letter (incorporating a small drawing) reproduced on one side of
leaf of paper watermarked "J WHATMAN 1912."
Notes: 50 numbered copies with manuscript limitation statement inscribed
and signed by Walker. Reproduced (and dated to December 1897) in *Some
Unknown Drawings of Aubrey Beardsley,* checklist no. 170, and in *Letters from
Aubrey Beardsley to Leonard Smithers,* checklist no. 184. The text is published
in *Letters,* where the letter is precisely dated to "[4 December 1897]."

159. **Stuart Mason [Christopher Sclater Millard]**
BIBLIOGRAPHY OF OSCAR WILDE. London: T. Werner Lau-
rie, [1914].
By Beardsley: Frontispiece, "Oscar Wilde at Work," a caricature of Wilde.
Reprinted in *The Uncollected Work,* checklist no. 177.
Blue cloth.   [G 775]
Notes: Front cover with design by Charles Ricketts (ornaments repeated on

---

[168] The composition of the exhibition changed with each venue, and the contents of the "Catalogue" were altered accordingly, along with the title-page, fly-title (p. 17), and front cover. An
"Additions and Errata" slip, noting the inclusion of one drawing and the omission of three, is
found in the Buffalo version.
[169] Such a large run is uncharacteristic of Evans's photographic reproductions of Beardsley's
work, the extent of which, however, has not yet been fully determined. He issued copies of various drawings for *Le Morte Darthur* and "A Facsimile" (1925, 25 "proofs" inscribed by Evans on
paper folder) of a peacock design [G 968] found in *The Uncollected Work,* checklist no. 177.

paste-down endpapers), first used on the 1905 limited edition of *De Profundis* [M p. 507], later on Lane's 1912 *Salome,* checklist no. 59 K. Other bindings include a plain red cloth necessitated by World War I shortages. A facsimile, styled a new edition, with an introduction by Timothy d'Arch Smith, was published by Bertram Rota, London, in 1967.

160. CATALOGUE OF THE BEARDSLEY-GARRIDO-GOFF EXHIBITION. Brighton: County Borough of Brighton Public Art Galleries, 12 December 1914–9 January 1915.
Grey wrappers. [G pp. 124–25]
Notes: Lists 82 drawings. Introductory note by Henry D. Roberts. Contains list of books relating to Beardsley in the Brighton Public Library.

161. AN EXHIBITION OF ORIGINAL DRAWINGS AND WATER COLORS BY MODERN ILLUSTRATORS. New York: James F. Drake, [ca. 1915].
By Beardsley: Front cover reproduces preliminary title-page design for the Bon-Mots Series.
Cream wrappers. [G 774]

162. **Aubrey Beardsley**
KRESBY A VERSE. Prelozil Jarmil Krecar. Bradac: Kral Vinohrady, 1916.
By Beardsley: Six drawings.
Parchment-backed grey boards.
Notes: Czech translations of "The Ballad of a Barber," "The Three Musicians," and Beardsley's version of Catullus's "Carmen CI."

163. **Aubrey Beardsley**
THE BALLAD OF A BARBER. [Regensburg: Privately printed in the order of Hermann Kruse in Wolgast at the office of Heinrich Schiele], 1919.
By Beardsley: "The Ballad of a Barber" and the accompanying two drawings from *The Savoy,* checklist no. 103.
Black boards. [G p. 108]
Notes: 265 numbered copies. Probably the first separate edition of the poem.

164. FORTY-THREE ORIGINAL DRAWINGS BY AUBREY BEARDSLEY. The collection of Frederick H. Evans of London. New York: Anderson Galleries, 20 March 1919.
Cream wrappers. [G p. 125]
Notes: Lists 43 drawings. Anderson Galleries Sale No. 1411.

165. AN EXHIBITION OF ORIGINAL DRAWINGS BY
AUBREY BEARDSLEY. With a foreword by Joseph Pennell. Philadelphia: Rosenbach Galleries, 1–17 May 1919.
Grey wrappers. [G p. 125]
Notes: Lists 25 drawings (most purchased at the Evans sale, checklist no.
164), also books, proofs, posters, four autograph letters, and the manuscript
of "Under the Hill." Front cover adapted from border design for *Le Morte
Darthur.* Pennell's foreword comprises an extract from his article in *The Studio,* April 1893, checklist no. 16, and a postscript dated April 1919.

166. **Aubrey Beardsley**
NINETEEN EARLY DRAWINGS BY AUBREY BEARDS-
LEY. From the collection of Mr. Harold Hartley of Brook House, North
Stoke, S. Oxon. With an introduction by Georges Derry. [London?:] Pri-
vately printed, 1919.[170]
By Beardsley: 19 previously unpublished comic illustrations to Book 11 of Vir-
gil's *Aeneid,* executed in late 1886.
Loose collotype plates, with separate, smaller-sized eight-page pamphlet, in
grey cloth-backed portfolio. [G 43–61 and p. 80; V 4]
Notes: Published in October 1919. 150 numbered copies signed by Hartley at
end of pamphlet, which contains an introduction by R. A. Walker under his
pseudonym Georges Derry.

167. THE BOOKPLATE BOOKLET. Kansas City, Mo. Vol. 1, No. 2, Oc-
tober 1919.
By Beardsley: Bookplate for John Lumsden Propert in article, "The Book-
Plates of Aubrey Beardsley," by Georges Derry [R. A. Walker].
Cream wrappers.
Notes: Includes a checklist of bookplates, and reproduces three bookplates
(for H. F. W. Manners-Sutton, John Henry Ashworth, and R. A. Walker)
adapted from Beardsley drawings. Walker has written elsewhere that of the
artist's work, "only three designs can be definitely and certainly ascribed as
Book-plates," specifically those for John Lumsden Propert, Herbert Charles
Pollitt, and Olive Custance, checklist nos. 51, 113, and 118.[171]

---

[170] Title printed on front cover of separate pamphlet.

[171] *An Aubrey Beardsley Lecture,* checklist no. 174, p. 42. Various drawings have been adapted for
bookplates by, among others, Frederick H. Evans (two designs, from *Le Morte Darthur*), Gerald
Kelly, Aleister Crowley, Frederick H. Charlier, H. F. W. Manners-Sutton, J. A. Hammerton,
William West, R. Norman McKibben, R. A. Walker (three designs), and John Henry Ash-
worth (Smithers's "chief assistant"). None of the plates in *Art Nouveau Bookplates by Aubrey
Beardsley,* by Dover Publications, New York (1976), are adapted from true bookplate designs.

168. AUBREY BEARDSLEY: LOAN EXHIBITION OF ORIGI-
NAL DRAWINGS. New York: Galleries of E. Gimpel and Wildenstein,
12 April–1 May 1920.

ORDINARY ISSUE   [G p. 126]
White wrappers.

SPECIAL ISSUE   [G 630 and p. 126; R 159; R & D 204]
By Beardsley: Frontispiece, previously unpublished chapter heading for *Le
Morte Darthur,* not found in ordinary issue.
Cream cloth-backed grey boards, glassine wrapper. 20 numbered copies
printed on handmade paper signed by A. E. Gallatin.

Notes: Lists 38 drawings. Preface by A. E. Gallatin. Front cover design
adapted from front cover for *The Life and Times of Madame du Barry,* checklist no. 104.

169. **Georges Derry [Rainforth Armitage Walker]**
AN AUBREY BEARDSLEY SCRAP BOOK. With an illustration
to Ibsen's "Ghosts." [London:] R. A. Walker, 1920.
By Beardsley: Frontispiece, previously unpublished drawing (ca. 1890) for
Henrik Ibsen's *Ghosts* (found in scrapbook described in this pamphlet).
Brown wrappers.   [G 165 and p. 81; R 18; R & D 102]
Notes: Published in January 1920. 200 numbered copies with manuscript
limitation statement signed by Walker as Derry.

170. **R[ainforth]. A[rmitage]. Walker**
SOME UNKNOWN DRAWINGS OF AUBREY BEARDS-
LEY. Collected and annotated by R. A. Walker (Georges Derry). London:
R. A. Walker, 1923.
By Beardsley: 13 drawings, nine published for the first time; also *A Caprice*
(1894), one of only two known oil paintings by the artist, and facsimiles of
three letters (two with sketches).
Cream cloth, dust jacket. [G 778, 780, and p. 81; R 323, 336; R & D 134, 476]
Notes: Published in October 1923. 500 numbered copies (450 for sale) signed
by Walker. Not all these drawings were "unknown"; also contains works by
others, including a sketch of the artist's grandfather, Surgeon-Major William
Pitt (possibly worked on by Beardsley), pastiches of his style (by Linley Sam-
bourne and E. T. Reed), and portraits and caricatures (by Rothenstein, Frederick Hollyer, Charles Conder, and Jacques-Emile Blanche).

171. CATALOGUE: LOAN EXHIBITION OF DRAWINGS BY
AUBREY BEARDSLEY (1872–1898). [London:] National Gallery,
Millbank, 1 November 1923–1 March 1924.
Yellow wrappers.   [G p. 126]

Notes: Lists 51 drawings and a painting by Beardsley, also portraits by Walter Sickert and Rothenstein and a caricature by Beerbohm. Introduction and entries by R. A. Walker.

172. CATALOGUE OF AN EXHIBITION OF ORIGINAL DRAWINGS BY AUBREY BEARDSLEY. [New York:] Brooklyn Museum, 19 December 1923–31 January 1924.
Grey wrappers. [G p. 127]
Notes: Lists 115 drawings. Introductory essay by Joseph Pennell comprises an extract from his article in *The Studio,* April 1893, checklist no. 16, a "Postscript" dated April 1919, and a new "Envoy" dated November 1923.

173. **Giovanni Boccaccio**
PASQUVERELLA AND MADONNA BABETTA. Two hitherto untranslated stories by Giovanni Boccaccio. With some hitherto unpublished sketches by Aubrey Beardsley. New York: Biblion Society, [1927].
By Beardsley: Frontispiece, six drawings, and text illustrations.
Black boards, printed label on spine, dust jacket.
Notes: 300 copies. The "hitherto unpublished sketches," which include a drawing for *Lysistrata* and chapter headings from *Le Morte Darthur,* had all been reproduced previously. None of the drawings relate to the text.

174. **A[rthur]. W[illiam]. King**
AN AUBREY BEARDSLEY LECTURE. With an introduction & notes by R. A. Walker and some unpublished letters & drawings. London: R. A. Walker, 1924.
By Beardsley: 16 previously unpublished letters (some in facsimile) to A. W. King, and 14 separate sketches (reproduced on plates).
Light blue boards, stamped label on spine. [G 11–32]
Notes: Published in November 1924. 500 copies (450 for sale) numbered and signed by Walker. The main text consists of a talk about Beardsley by King.

175. **Joseph Pennell**
AUBREY BEARDSLEY AND OTHER MEN OF THE NINETIES. Lecture delivered at the Brooklyn Museum of Science and Art on the occasion of the Beardsley exhibition, November 1923. Philadelphia: Privately printed for the Pennell Club, 1924.
By Beardsley: Frontispiece, "Raphael Sanzio" (not first publication as stated).
Yellow boards, cloth dust jacket. [G p. 78]
Notes: 100 numbered copies. Vol. III of the Pennell Club's publications, a lecture delivered at the Brooklyn Museum Beardsley exhibition, checklist no. 172. Title-page vignette designed by Pennell.

176. **E[van]. H[illhouse]. M[ethuen]. Cox,** comp.
THE LIBRARY OF EDMUND GOSSE. Being a descriptive and
bibliographical catalogue of a portion of his collection. With an introductory
essay by Mr. Gosse. London: Dulau & Company, 1924.
By Beardsley: Two previously unpublished letters, the first to Lady Henrietta
Pelham, 1 February [1883?], the second to Gosse [ca. 5 May 1896, sending
the dedication copy of *The Rape of the Lock*]. Both reprinted in *Letters.*
Blue cloth, dust jacket.

177. **Aubrey Beardsley**
THE UNCOLLECTED WORK OF AUBREY BEARDSLEY.
With an introduction by C. Lewis Hind. London: John Lane, [1925].
By Beardsley: 154 drawings, facsimiles of letters, etc., some published for the
first time.[172]

ORDINARY ISSUE   [G p. 75]
Cream cloth (also blue cloth), dust jacket.

SPECIAL ISSUE   [G p. 75]
By Beardsley: Six additional drawings not in ordinary issue, bound in or as
loose plates in separate portfolio: five from *An Issue of Five Drawings Illustra-*
tive of Juvenal and Lucian, checklist no. 149, and the variant version of "A
Snare of Vintage," first included in the special issue of *Lucian's True History,*
checklist no. 78.
Cream cloth stamped in gilt. 110 numbered copies printed on Japan vellum.

Notes: Published 10 July 1925. Also contains a caricature by Max Beerbohm.
Front cover design, spine ornament, and title-page design are from *The Early*
Work, checklist no. 133, and from *The Later Work,* checklist no. 136. Copies
sold in the U.S. have the name of Dodd, Mead at foot of spine.

178. THE JOHN LANE COLLECTION OF ORIGINAL DRAW-
INGS BY AUBREY BEARDSLEY. Sold by order of Mrs. John Lane,
London, England. New York: Anderson Galleries, 22 November 1926.
By Beardsley: 16 drawings, including previously unpublished juvenile sketch,
"Xmas Eve at Din[g]ley Dell," an illustration to Dickens's *Pickwick Papers.*
Cream wrappers.   [G 124 and p. 127]
Notes: Lists 87 drawings in 57 lots. Preface by Guy Eglington. Anderson
Galleries Sale No. 2104.

---

[172] According to Gallatin, the "42 tiny sketches" reproduced on Pls. 44–47 are *not* by Beardsley.

179. **[Chambers] Haldane Macfall**
AUBREY BEARDSLEY. The clown, the harlequin, the pierrot of his
age. New York: Simon and Schuster, 1927.
By Beardsley: 53 drawings, and an untitled limerick about the drawings for *Le
Morte Darthur.* [173]

LARGE PAPER ISSUE   [G pp. 77–78]
Black cloth, slipcase. 300 numbered copies signed by Macfall.
Notes: Said by Gallatin to precede the ordinary issue.

ORDINARY ISSUE   [G pp. 77–78]
Black cloth.

Notes: Front cover reproduces front cover ornament from first edition of
Salome, checklist no. 59.

179A. AUBREY BEARDSLEY. The man and his work. London: John
Lane, [1928].

ORDINARY ISSUE   [G p. 78]
Green cloth-backed green boards, printed label on spine, dust jacket.

SPECIAL ISSUE
By Beardsley: Five drawings not in ordinary issue (contributions to the ill-
fated Vol. v of *The Yellow Book,* and "Venus"), and facsimile of letter to John
Lane [March 1894] with self-portrait pointing to a hangman's noose.
White cloth, printed label on spine. 100 numbered copies.[174]

Notes: Published in March 1928. Reprints of the ordinary issue were published by Folcroft Library Editions, Folcroft, Pa., in 1971, by Books for Libraries Press, Freeport, N. Y., in 1972, by Norwood Editions, Norwood, Pa.,
in 1976, and by R. West, Philadelphia, in 1977.

180. CATALOGUE NUMBER 165: BOOKS FROM THE LI-
BRARY OF JOHN LANE, PUBLISHER. Including first editions
and mss. of modern authors. Also first editions of the nineties privately purchased from a gentleman's library. London: Dulau and Company, [1929].
By Beardsley: Extracts from 13 letters (mostly to John Lane) and a stanza from
a poem lampooning Gladstone's government.
Yellow wrappers.   [G p. 94]

---

[173] A variant version appeared in Malcolm Easton, *Aubrey and the Dying Lady,* checklist no. 202.
[174] One copy examined is signed "Haldane Macfall" below the limitation notice, but the signature is markedly different from the handwriting found in the American large paper issue and
does not resemble Macfall's usual calligraphic hand.

Notes: Lists many items by or relating to Beardsley, including original drawings and other letters, which are paraphrased, not quoted.

181. CATALOGUE NO. 170: THE CHOICE & REMARKABLY
EXTENSIVE AUBREY BEARDSLEY COLLECTION AS-
SEMBLED BY THE LATE PICKFORD WALLER. Together
with first editions & finely illustrated books, both modern and of a period
more remote; and some sets of unusual literary magazines & periodicals,
both staid & unconventional, of much interest to the collector. From the
same source. London: Frank Hollings, 1931.
Cream wrappers.
Notes: The first 97 listings (some including multiple items) are by or about
Beardsley. Includes descriptions of a few original drawings.

182. **William Rothenstein**
MEN AND MEMORIES. Recollections of William Rothenstein,
1872–1900. London: Faber & Faber, [1931].
By Beardsley: One letter and extracts from two letters to Rothenstein, all re-
printed in *Letters,* and facsimile of manuscript of poem, "The Three Musi-
cians."
Black cloth, dust jacket.   [G p. 90]
Notes: Published in February 1931.

183. **J. Lewis May**
JOHN LANE AND THE NINETIES. London: John Lane, [1936].
By Beardsley: Six drawings, and extracts from letter to G. F. Scotson-Clark
[July 1891] and from three letters to Lane (including one with self-portrait
pointing to a hangman's noose, reproduced in part, and another [12 Septem-
ber 1893] with self-portrait and caricatures of Lane and Rothenstein, repro-
duced in full). Texts of the letters reprinted in *Letters.*
Red cloth, dust jacket.

184. **Aubrey Beardsley**
LETTERS FROM AUBREY BEARDSLEY TO LEONARD
SMITHERS. Edited with introduction and notes by R. A. Walker. [Lon-
don:] The First Edition Club, 1937.
By Beardsley: 186 letters to Smithers, plus one to Ernest Dowson and one to
J. H. Ashworth.
Black cloth.   [G 777 and pp. 118–20]
Notes: Published in June 1937. "To the Waerndorfer letters are added 16 oth-
ers, as well as extracts from a further 8, but 11 letters published in the 1908

German edition [*Briefe,* checklist no. 152] were no longer in the collection...."[175] Title-page reproduces a previously unpublished drawing (1894) intended for *The Idler.*

185. AUBREY BEARDSLEY: EXHIBITION OF DRAWINGS &
BOOKS. New York: The Grolier Club, 16 March–10 April 1945.
By Beardsley: "The Rape of the Lock" reproduced on first page.
Folded leaf.   [G pp. 127–28]
Notes: Lists books and 40 drawings, the majority lent by A. E. Gallatin.[176]

186. **A[lbert]. E[ugene]. Gallatin**
AUBREY BEARDSLEY: CATALOGUE OF DRAWINGS
AND BIBLIOGRAPHY. New York: The Grolier Club, 1945.
By Beardsley: Seven drawings, five published for the first time; the latter comprised: sketch in Beardsley's copy of Jonathan Swift's *Prose Writings* (1886), "Sarah Bernhardt," initial letter "J" intended for *Le Morte Darthur,* grotesque intended for the Bon-Mots Series, and "Carl Maria von Weber." Also reprints Beardsley's contribution to "The Art of the Hoarding" and a letter to the editor of the *Daily Chronicle,* 17 April 1894, checklist nos. 71 and 66.
Dark blue cloth, dust jacket. [G 67, 167, 628, 773, 776; R 12, 29, 160, 251;
R & D 128, 201, 234; V 59 XXII]
Notes: 300 copies. Reprinted by Paul P. Appel, Mamaroneck, N. Y., in 1980.

187. **Derek Hudson**
NORMAN O'NEILL. A life of music. London: Quality Press, [1945].
By Beardsley: Three previously unpublished caricatures of Norman O'Neill.[177]
Blue cloth, dust jacket.   [G 846–48; R 53–54; R & D 143–44]
Notes: Published in June 1945.

188. **R[ainforth]. A[rmitage]. Walker**
LE MORTE DARTHUR WITH BEARDSLEY ILLUSTRA-
TIONS. A bibliographical essay. Bedford: Published by the author, 1945.
Grey wrappers.
Notes: 350 copies. Bibliographical description of *Le Morte Darthur,* contrasting it to the work of the Kelmscott Press. Expanded from "Bibliographical Notes on 'Le Morte d'Arthur,'" *TLS,* 31 March 1945 [G p. 92].

---

[175] Warrack and Perkins 136.
[176] At the meeting of the Grolier Club on 15 March 1945, J. Harlin O'Connell spoke on "Aubrey Beardsley and the Men of the Nineties."
[177] From a series of four entitled "The English Flower in the German Conservatory" depicting O'Neill as a music student in Frankfurt, captioned by Count Eric Stenbock; see Adlard, p. 54.

189. **Aubrey Beardsley**
THE BEST OF BEARDSLEY. Collected and edited by R. A. Walker.
London: The Bodley Head, [1948].
By Beardsley: 134 drawings, one of which, the original version of "Enter
Herodias," is published for the first time.
Yellow cloth, dust jacket.
Notes: Published in October 1948. Front cover design adapted from cover for
Volpone, checklist no. 129. Reprinted in 1956? by Spring Books, London, and
in 1983 by Chancellor, London and Excalibur, New York.

190. **Aubrey Beardsley**
A BEARDSLEY MISCELLANY. Selected and edited by R. A.
Walker. London: The Bodley Head, [1949].
By Beardsley: 12 drawings, including a self-portrait from a letter and the pre-
viously unpublished "Il était une Bergère." Also includes Beardsley's contri-
bution to "The Art of the Hoarding," checklist no. 71, a variant text of *The
Story of Venus and Tannhäuser* (one page of manuscript reproduced), and fac-
similes of manuscripts of "The Ballad of a Barber," of the prospectus for
Volpone, checklist no. 129A, and of the previously unpublished poem, "The
Ivory Piece."
Black cloth, dust jacket.
Notes: Published in August 1949. 500 numbered copies. Frontispiece is a
previously unpublished caricature of Beardsley by Max Beerbohm; the book
also contains reminiscences by the artist's mother, Ellen Agnus Beardsley.
Front cover design (repeated on dust jacket) adapted from cover for the "Bi-
jou" edition of *The Rape of the Lock,* checklist no. 105A.

191. QUARTO 8: AUBREY BEARDSLEY. Some items from the collec-
tion of R. A. Walker. Bishops Stortford: Elkin Mathews Ltd., May 1950.
Stapled (first leaf made of yellow paper).
Notes: Lists 86 items by or relating to Beardsley, including 12 original draw-
ings. First leaf reproduces a drawing intended for *The Idler,* first published in
Letters from Aubrey Beardsley to Leonard Smithers, checklist no. 184.

192. **R[ainforth]. A[rmitage]. Walker**
HOW TO DETECT BEARDSLEY FORGERIES. Bedford: R. A.
Walker, 1950.
By Beardsley: Two drawings and enlarged reproduction of details.
Grey wrappers.
Notes: Published in April 1950. 250 copies. Four forgeries are also repro-
duced. The appendix contains a descriptive list of spurious works.

193. A[lbert]. E[ugene]. Gallatin and Alexander D. Wainwright
THE GALLATIN BEARDSLEY COLLECTION IN THE
PRINCETON UNIVERSITY LIBRARY. A catalogue compiled by
A. E. Gallatin and Alexander D. Wainwright. Princeton: Princeton University
Library, 1952.
By Beardsley: Five drawings, including two sketches in letters.
Tan wrappers.
Notes: First appearing in three separate issues of *The Princeton University Library Chronicle,* 1949–51, this descriptive catalogue includes an extensive list
of letters and several previously unpublished extracts.[178] Front cover design
adapted from title-page and cover for *Yellow and White,* checklist no. 40.

194. **Margery Ross,** ed.
ROBERT ROSS. Friend of friends. Letters to Robert Ross, art critic and
writer, together with extracts from his published articles. London: Jonathan
Cape, [1952].
By Beardsley: 12 previously unpublished letters to Ross (one reproduced in
facsimile), and an unpublished sketch drawn on an envelope.
Blue-green cloth, dust jacket.
Notes: Published in March 1952.

195. **Aubrey Beardsley**
A LETTER TO SMITHERS. With a note by Patricio Gannon. Edinburgh: Tragara Press, 1963.
By Beardsley: Previously unpublished letter to Leonard Smithers [18 September 1897]. Reprinted in *Letters.*
Cream wrappers.
Notes: 55 numbered copies. Front cover reproduces cover (called in letter "the
pig and the pillar" drawing) for *The Houses of Sin,* checklist no. 120.

196. **Brian Reade and Frank Dickinson**
AUBREY BEARDSLEY EXHIBITION AT THE VICTORIA
AND ALBERT MUSEUM. Catalogue of the original drawings, letters,
manuscripts, paintings, and of books, posters, photographs, documents, etc.
[London: Her Majesty's Stationery Office], 1966.
By Beardsley: Extracts from previously unpublished letters and documents.
Green wrappers.

---

[178] Additions to the collection are described in articles in *The Princeton University Library Chronicle:* J. Benjamin Townsend, "The Yellow Book" (Winter 1955), pp. 101–3; R. A. Walker, "Letters of Aubrey Beardsley" (Spring 1955), pp. 111–44 (full texts of 60 letters, three sketches from letters reproduced); "Addendum to the Beardsley Collection" (Winter 1958), pp. 104–5; and Robert H. Taylor, "The J. Harlin O'Connell Collection" (Spring-Summer 1958), pp. 149–52.

Notes: Lists 611 items by or relating to Beardsley. Versions of this exhibition were held in New York (1967), checklist no. 196B; Los Angeles (1967–68); Japan (1983), checklist no. 196C; Munich (1984), checklist no. 196D; Salzburg (1984–85); Rome (1985), checklist no. 196E; and Milan (1985).

196A. **Brian Reade**
AUBREY BEARDSLEY. London: Her Majesty's Stationery Office, 1966.
By Beardsley: 59 drawings.
Grey wrappers.
Notes: Victoria and Albert Museum Large Picture Book No. 32, published in connection with 1966 London exhibition, checklist no. 196. Distributed also with copies of the catalogue for 1967 New York version of the show, checklist no. 196B, and reprinted several times.[179] Front cover and title-page design reproduce that for *The Dancing Faun,* checklist no. 26.

196B. AUBREY BEARDSLEY. An exhibition arranged by Brian Reade for the Gallery of Modern Art including the Huntington Hartford collection. [New York: Gallery of Modern Art], 14 February–9 April 1967.
By Beardsley: Extracts from letters and documents.
Cream wrappers.
Notes: Describes smaller version (508 items) of 1966 London exhibition, checklist no. 196. Copies were also issued with Brian Reade's *Aubrey Beardsley* essay-and-picture book, checklist no. 196A, in a cream folder/slipcase.

196C. AUBREY BEARDSLEY. 1872–1898. An exhibition of prints, drawings, and books from the Victoria & Albert Museum and other collections. [Tokyo: Tokyo Shinbun, 1983].[180]
By Beardsley: 262 drawings, posters, pages from books, book covers, etc.
White wrappers.
Notes: Describes version of 1966 London exhibition, checklist no. 196, with loans from other sources. The exhibition began at the Isetan Museum of Art, Tokyo, 16–28 June 1983, and traveled to Osaka, Okazaki, and Funabashi. Text in Japanese. Contains essay (also in English), "Aubrey Beardsley and Japan" by Brian Reade, and many excellent color reproductions of posters and book covers. Illustrations also include works by imitators of Beardsley and photographs of the artist and his circle. Front cover reproduces "Isolde," checklist no. 91, and back cover reproduces pierrot design from invitation card for John Lane's Sette of Odd Volumes "Smoke," checklist no. 83.

---

[179] The fifth impression (1972) takes account in the list of plates of recent changes of ownership.
[180] Title from preliminary leaf.

196D. AUBREY BEARDSLEY IN DEN "YELLOW NINE-TIES." 1891–1898. Dekadenz oder Modernität. [Munich?:] Museum Villa Stuck, 27 September–25 November 1984.
By Beardsley: 128 drawings, posters, pages from books, book covers, etc.
Yellow wrappers.
Notes: Describes version of 1966 London exhibition, checklist no. 196. Text in German. Contains a chronology; biography; essays by Rüdiger Maria Kampmann; commentaries by Kenneth Clark, Brigid Brophy, Arthur Symons, Franz Blei, and Hans A. Halbey; detailed entries; and a bibliography. Illustrations include photographs of Beardsley and his family and friends. Front cover adapted from design for prospectus for Vol. 1 of *The Yellow Book,* checklist no. 65A; back cover reproduces tailpiece from *Salome.*

196E. AUBREY BEARDSLEY. 1872 [–] 1898. Soprintendenza Speciale alla Galleria Nazionale d'Arte Moderna e Contemporanea. Rome: Fratelli Palombi Editori, 13 March–28 April 1985.
By Beardsley: 197 drawings, posters, pages from books, book covers, etc.
Silver wrappers.
Notes: Describes version of 1966 London exhibition, checklist no. 196. Text in Italian. Contains an introduction by Brian Reade, a chronology, and a bibliography. Illustrations include works by imitators of Beardsley. Front cover reproduces pierrot design from invitation card for John Lane's Sette of Odd Volumes "Smoke," checklist no. 83; back cover reproduces self-portrait silhouette from *A Book of Fifty Drawings,* checklist no. 112.

196F. AUBREY BEARDSLEY. 1872–1898. [Milan:] Mazzotta, [17 May–16 June 1985].
By Beardsley: 336 drawings, posters, pages from books, book covers, etc.[181]
White wrappers.
Notes: Describes version of 1966 London exhibition, checklist no. 196, held at Palazzo Bagatti Valsecchi, Milan. Text in Italian. Contains essays by Renato Barilli and Federica Di Castro. Front cover reproduces design for Smithers's catalogue of rare books, checklist no. 96.

197. **Aubrey Beardsley**
THE COLLECTED DRAWINGS OF AUBREY BEARDS-LEY. With an appreciation by Arthur Symons. Edited by Bruce S. Harris. New York: Crescent Books, [1967].
White cloth-backed grey boards, dust jacket.
By Beardsley: 79 drawings, pages from books, book covers, etc.

---

[181] The catalogue also reproduces 36 sketches from *The Uncollected Work,* checklist no. 177, which Gallatin (p. 75) has stated are not by Beardsley.

Notes: Also reprints 47 drawings from *Fifty Drawings by Aubrey Beardsley,* checklist no. 222—properly described as spurious—and the title-page and forgery, "Adoration of the Penis," from the Beardsley Press edition of *Lysistrata,* checklist no. 107c.[182] Symons's text is from the first edition of his *Aubrey Beardsley,* checklist no. 130.

198. **Brian Reade**
BEARDSLEY. Introduction by John Rothenstein. London: Studio Vista, [1967].
By Beardsley: 503 drawings, posters, pages from books, book covers, etc., some published for the first time.
Green cloth, dust jacket.
Notes: The most comprehensive album of Beardsley's work. An American issue, *Aubrey Beardsley,* was published the same year by Viking Press, New York, and reprinted [1974?] by a Viking subsidiary, Bonanza Books. In 1987 a revised impression with minor changes (and without Rothenstein's introduction) was issued by the Antique Collectors' Club, Woodbridge, England.

199. **Stanley Weintraub**
BEARDSLEY. A biography. New York: George Braziller, [1967].
By Beardsley: 16 drawings, pages from books, etc., and extracts from previously unpublished letters.
Pale yellow cloth, dust jacket.
Notes: An English issue was published the same year by W. H. Allen, London. In 1972 Penguin Books, Harmondsworth, published a revised paperback edition. Max Beerbohm's essay, "Ex Cathedra v: Mr. Beardsley's Fifty Drawings," which originally appeared in *To-Morrow,* January 1897, is printed as an appendix. A German translation (by Christian Spiel) was published by Winkler-Verlag, Munich, in 1968.[183]

199A. AUBREY BEARDSLEY. Imp of the perverse. University Park, Pa.: Pennsylvania State University Press, [1976].
By Beardsley: 150 drawings, pages from books, etc.
Black cloth, dust jacket (also as paperback, wrappers printed same as jacket).
Notes: A revised version of the 1967 biography, checklist no. 199, with additional previously unpublished material—virtually a different book.[184]

---

[182] Front cover of *The Collected Drawings,* adapted from another Nichols forgery, is found again on a reprint published by Bounty Books, New York. Another Bounty version has a plain cover.
[183] This translation omits the Beerbohm essay.
[184] It might even be called newly unexpurgated: "An editor involved in the publication of the earlier life [1967] cautiously put aside certain relevant textual and pictorial material on grounds that 'lady librarians' would be repelled, and sales would thus suffer" (Author's Note, p. ix).

200. **Brigid Brophy**
BLACK AND WHITE. A portrait of Aubrey Beardsley. London: Jonathan Cape, 1968.
By Beardsley: 44 drawings.
Black cloth, dust jacket.
Notes: Short study with chronology, not to be confused with Brophy's *Beardsley and His World,* checklist no. 204. An American issue was published by Stein and Day, New York, in 1969.

201. **Aubrey Beardsley**
THE LETTERS OF AUBREY BEARDSLEY. Edited by Henry Maas, J. L. Duncan, and W. G. Good. Rutherford, N. J.: Fairleigh Dickinson University Press, [1970].
By Beardsley: 631 letters (seven with sketches reproduced in whole or in part) and three drawings, one published for the first time.
Black cloth, dust jacket.
Notes: Includes two letters from Mabel Beardsley and one from the artist's mother, Ellen Agnus Beardsley. An English issue was published the same year by Cassell, London, and a paperback version was brought out by Plantin, Deddington, Oxfordshire, in 1990.

202. **Malcolm Easton**
AUBREY AND THE DYING LADY. A Beardsley riddle. London: Secker and Warburg, 1972.
By Beardsley: 53 drawings, pages from books, book covers, etc., and facsimiles of two letters.
Black cloth, dust jacket.
Notes: Contains previously unpublished documents by Beardsley's circle. Title-page adapted from front cover of Vol. III of *The Yellow Book.* An American issue was published the same year by David R. Godine, Boston.

203. **Kenneth Clark**
THE BEST OF AUBREY BEARDSLEY. New York: Doubleday, [1978].
By Beardsley: 66 drawings.
White cloth, dust jacket.
Notes: An English edition was published by John Murray, London, in 1979.

204. **Brigid Brophy**
BEARDSLEY AND HIS WORLD. London: Thames and Hudson, [1976].
By Beardsley: 64 drawings, posters, etc., and facsimiles of letters.
Yellow cloth, dust jacket.

Notes: Extensively illustrated biography, not to be confused with Brophy's earlier *Black and White,* checklist no. 200. An American issue was published the same year by Harmony Books, New York.

205. **Simon Wilson**
BEARDSLEY. [Oxford]: Phaidon, [1976].
By Beardsley: 54 drawings, pages from books, book covers, etc.
Black cloth, dust jacket.

205A. [NEW, ENLARGED EDITION]. Oxford: Phaidon, [1983].
By Beardsley: 89 drawings, pages from books, book covers, etc.
Black cloth, dust jacket.
Notes: Contains revised text. Also issued as a paperback, in yellow wrappers.

206. CATALOGUE NUMBER 44: AUBREY BEARDSLEY. Chicago: J. Stephan Lawrence, Rare Books, [1979].
By Beardsley: 39 drawings, posters, pages from books, book covers, etc., including four juvenile drawings ("Ici On Parle Français") and the text of a letter [ca. 1895] to Frederic Chapman, John Lane's manager at the Bodley Head, all published for the first time.
Cream wrappers. [G 89–92]
Notes: Lists 144 items by or about Beardsley. Front cover reproduces "The Fourth Tableau of Das Rheingold," cover design for *The Savoy,* No. 6, checklist no. 103; back cover reproduces a grotesque from the Bon-Mots Series.

207. **John Gray**
AUBREY BEARDSLEY. An obituary memoir. Translated from the French. Edinburgh: Privately printed [by Alan Anderson at the Tragara Press], 1980.
Grey wrappers.
Notes: 95 numbered copies. Gray's article first appeared in *La Revue Blanche* in 1898. Frontispiece reproduces a portrait of Beardsley by Félix Vallotton.

208. **Miriam J. Benkovitz**
AUBREY BEARDSLEY. An account of his life. New York: G. P. Putnam's Sons, [1981].
By Beardsley: 24 drawings, pages from books, facsimiles of manuscripts, etc.
Black cloth, dust jacket.
Notes: Includes previously unpublished documents relating to Beardsley and his circle. Title-page design adapted from title-page for *Salome,* checklist no. 59. An English issue was published the same year by Hamish Hamilton, London.

209. CATALOGUE SIXTY: AUBREY BEARDSLEY. Church En-
stone, Oxfordshire: Warrack & Perkins, [1985].
By Beardsley: 51 drawings, pages from books, book covers, etc.; also facsimile
of a previously unpublished letter to Leonard Smithers and text of another.
Cream wrappers.
Notes: 350 copies. Lists 140 items by or relating to Beardsley. The illustrations include the front cover of the Stone and Kimball Poe portfolio, checklist no. 80, and two designs by Beardsley imitators. Front cover reproduces
cover for *Volpone,* checklist no. 129.

210. **David March**
D'ALBERT S'EXPOSE: AUBREY BEARDSLEY'S DRAW-
INGS FOR MADEMOISELLE DE MAUPIN. New York: David
March, 1985.
By Beardsley: Seven drawings and four details.
Grey wrappers, printed label on front cover.
Notes: 300 numbered copies. Printed by Dikko Faust. Text based on a chap-
ter of the author's unpublished M.A. thesis, "The Cosmetic Pow'rs: Toilette
Scenes by Aubrey Beardsley," University of Missouri, Columbia, 1975.

211. **Ian Fletcher**
AUBREY BEARDSLEY. Boston: Twayne Publishers, [1987].
Scarlet cloth, dust jacket.
Notes: A volume in Twayne's English Authors Series. No illustrations.

212. **David March**
PRIAPUSA: MANICURE & FARDEUSE. Or the reine des ribauds in
the land of the queen of love. New York: [David March], 1988.
By Beardsley: Three drawings.
Mint green wrappers, printed label on front cover.
Notes: 150 copies numbered and signed by March. Printed by Dikko Faust.
A study of *The Story of Venus and Tannhäuser.*

213. **Brian Reade**
BEARDSLEY RE-MOUNTED. London: Eighteen Nineties Society,
[1989].
By Beardsley: Three drawings.
Blue cloth, dust jacket.
Notes: Reprinted in *Reconsidering Aubrey Beardsley,* checklist no. 214. Also
contains a previously unpublished sketch of Beardsley by Kate Oliver. Front
cover adapted from "Apollo Pursuing Daphne" [R 455].

214. **Robert Langenfeld**, ed.
RECONSIDERING AUBREY BEARDSLEY. With an annotated
secondary bibliography by Nicholas Salerno. Foreword by Simon Wilson.
Ann Arbor, Mich.: UMI Research Press, [1989].
By Beardsley: 65 drawings, posters, pages from books, etc., including self-portrait sketch from a letter. An extract from the juvenile poem, "A Ride on an
Omnibus," and two unfinished works, the poem "The Ivory Piece" and the
prose "The Celestial Love" (both 1898), in Ian Fletcher's essay, "Inventions
for the Left Hand: Beardsley in Verse and Prose."
Red cloth, dust jacket.
Notes: A collection of critical essays, with contributions by Robert Langenfeld, Chris Snodgrass, John Stokes, Bridget J. Elliot, Brian Reade (see
checklist no. 213), Rodney Shewan, Linda Zatlin, Karl Beckson, and Ian
Fletcher. Nicholas Salerno's secondary bibliography (prefaced by an analysis
of Beardsley literature) runs to 1,561 items, encompassing books, articles, dis-
sertations, catalogues, and reviews.

215. **Linda Gertner Zatlin**
AUBREY BEARDSLEY AND VICTORIAN SEXUAL POLI-
TICS. Oxford: Clarendon Press, 1990.
By Beardsley: 108 drawings, pages from books, etc.
Black cloth, dust jacket.

216. CATALOGUE 18: WILDE, BEARDSLEY, AND THE
EIGHTEEN-NINETIES. The collection of Giles Gordon. With a
foreword and afterword by Peter Ackroyd. [London:] Gekoski, Summer
1994.
By Beardsley: Four drawings, including two sketches of Beaumont and
Fletcher (1886, described in detail in Ackroyd's afterword) published for the
first time. Also contains facsimile of a letter to Ada Leverson and the corrected text of a letter to Leonard Smithers.

ORDINARY ISSUE
White wrappers. 750 copies. Front cover adapted from cover design for
Smithers's catalogue of rare books, checklist no. 96.

SPECIAL ISSUE
White wrappers, in slipcase. 26 lettered copies printed on green paper signed
by Peter Ackroyd.

Notes: Lists approximately 100 items by or relating to Beardsley.

A Note on Misattributions

There exist many forgeries of Beardsley's drawings. Most are fraudulent copies of genuine originals. Some are outright fakes, and still others might best be termed "pastiches," in which elements from existing works are combined to make a "new" image. Just who was responsible for specific deceptions is difficult to assess, the most likely culprits being three of Leonard Smithers's associates—John Black, Alfred Cooper,[185] and H[arry]. S[idney]. Nichols[186]—as well as possibly Smithers himself, and at least one American working in the period 1920–50. In his 1950 pamphlet, *How to Detect Beardsley Forgeries,* checklist no. 192, R. A. Walker gave detailed instructions on how to distinguish the wheat from the chaff, but even his guidelines are not foolproof. Provenance is, as always with artworks, of the greatest importance. Simply put, the authenticity of a purported Beardsley drawing without a credible history should be disbelieved until proven otherwise. (Inscriptions and Beardsley's signature in books should also be verified by experts.) This section lists the most infamous volume of published forgeries, *Fifty Drawings by Aubrey Beardsley,* and several books which contain work erroneously attributed to the artist.

217. **Arthur Rickett**[187]
LOST CHORDS. Some emotions without morals. London: A. D. Innes, 1895.
Contains: Title-page design (repeated on front cover) and spine design imitating Beardsley's Keynotes Series format.
Yellow cloth.   [R & D 54]
Notes: Rickett's text consists of parodies of such contemporary writers as George Egerton ("Miss Maud's Three Notes"), Victoria Crosse ("Golden Syrup"), Richard Le Gallienne ("Pose Fancies"), and Arthur Machen ("A Yellow Creeper"). The cover design "is signed with the initials T D or D T and may possibly be the work of the illustrator and caricaturist Thomas Downey, who was employed by journals such as The Sketch, the Daily Graphic, and The Idler in the Nineties."[188]

---

[185] Cooper traded as "Wright and Jones," the distributor of (among other piracies) the 1904 edition of *Salome,* checklist no. 59 B. See R & D 48, 496, and 535.
[186] See R & D 602.
[187] (1869–1937), who later added the middle, sometimes hyphenated, name of Compton to his title-pages. A minor man of letters, he is remembered—if at all—for this book (his first), for *The Vagabond in Literature* (1906), and for his co-editing, with Thomas Hake, of *The Life and Letters of Theodore Watts-Dunton* (1916).
[188] Warrack and Perkins, *Catalogue Sixty-Three: A Miscellany* [1987], item 4.

218. Menu for Sette of Odd Volumes dinner, Limmer's Hotel [London], 3 May
1895.
Contains: Portrait of Richard Le Gallienne, speculatively attributed to
Beardsley by an unnamed bookseller.
Folded leaf of grey paper.
Notes: Depicts Le Gallienne reading from a manuscript titled "On the Ideal
Aspects of the Collector." The portrait, though drawn in Beardsley's man-
ner, is not by him, nor is the drawing on the first panel, a sketch of a library
done in the manner of Dürer.

219. **Ernest Dowson**
DECORATIONS. In verse and prose. London: Leonard Smithers, 1899.
Contains: Cover design sometimes erroneously attributed to Beardsley.
Cream parchment.
Notes: Published ca. 25 October 1899. 300 copies. According to Dowson's
biographer and editor Mark Longaker, "Guy Harrison, who supplied the
bibliography for Victor Plarr's *Ernest Dowson* (1914), was in error in naming
Aubrey Beardsley as the designer of the cover."[189] Longaker attributes the entire design to the artist Althea Gyles,[190] whose monogram (an "A" within a
heart) is found only on the back cover. Other commentators have ascribed
the front cover to Pickford Waller.[191]

220. **Richard Le Gallienne**
THE ROMANCE OF ZION CHAPEL. London: John Lane, 1898.
Contains: Cover design sometimes erroneously attributed to Beardsley.
Black cloth.   [R & D 31]
Notes: First American edition (thought to precede the English), printed by
the University Press, Cambridge, Mass. R. J. C. Lingel, in his 1926 *A Bib-
liographical Checklist of the Writings of Richard Le Gallienne,* states that the
elaborate cover is by Beardsley.[192] In fact, the design is the work of Will H.
Bradley, the American typographer, book designer, and poster artist.

[189] Ernest Dowson, *The Poems of Ernest Dowson,* ed. Mark Longaker (1962), p. 230.
[190] (1868–1949), illustrator and writer, perhaps best known for her illustrations to Wilde's *The
Harlot's House* (1904) and cover designs for books by Yeats, among them *The Secret Rose* (1897)
and *The Wind Among the Reeds* (1898). See Bonnie J. Robinson, "Althea Gyles," *The 1890s: An
Encyclopedia of British Literature, Art, and Culture,* ed. G. A. Cevasco (1993), pp. 250–51.
[191] Colbeck, Vol. 1, p. 223; also C. A. and H. W. Stonehill, *Bibliographies of Modern Authors: Second Series* (1925), p. 59. An amateur artist, dramatist, and bookplate designer, Waller (1873–
1927) was also a collector of Beardsley's work; see checklist no. 181.
[192] R. J. C. Lingel, *A Bibliographical Checklist of the Writings of Richard Le Gallienne* (1926), p. 47.
Lingel's assertion is repeated by Richard Whittington-Egan and Geoffrey Smerdon, *The Quest
of the Gilt-Edged Boy: The Life and Letters of Richard Le Gallienne* (1960), p. 555.

221. **Simon Arrow**
COUNT FANNY'S NUPTIALS. Being the story of a courtship. [London:] Printed for private circulation, and published by G. G. Hope Johnstone, [1907].[193]
Contains: Seven unsigned drawings by Alastair [Hans Henning Voight].[194]
Navy blue cloth.   [R & D 49]
Notes: The illustrations are sometimes wrongly said to be by Beardsley. G. G. Hope Johnstone, the book's "publisher," probably wrote the text.[195]

222. FIFTY DRAWINGS BY AUBREY BEARDSLEY. Selected from the collection owned by Mr. H. S. Nichols. Published for subscribers only. New York: H. S. Nichols, 1920.
Contains: 50 drawings, all forgeries. 47 reprinted (as spurious works) in *The Collected Drawings of Aubrey Beardsley*, checklist no. 197.
Black cloth, dust jacket.   [G pp. 139–41; R & D 50]
Notes: 500 numbered copies signed by Nichols. The drawings, "exhibited, with 20 others, at Nichols' bookshop, 17 East 33rd Street, New York, 14–19 April 1919," were at once denounced by A. E. Gallatin and Joseph Pennell. According to Gallatin, Haldane Macfall believed them to be the work of "at least two forgers," probably Nichols and one of his associates.[196]

223. THE LUSTFUL TURK. Or scenes in the harem of an eastern potentate. Part 1. London: Printed for the Society of Vice, [ca. 1920–30].
Contains: Color illustrations signed "Beardsley" on scrolls, all obvious fakes.
Green morocco.

224. IN MEMORIAM: AUBREY VINCENT BEARDSLEY: 1872–1898. [ca. 1923?].
Contains: Drawing depicting Beardsley lying in bed surrounded by figures from his drawings, including Salome. Printed legend below.
Single leaf of card stock.
Notes: A clever pastiche, obviously not by Beardsley. Copy found inserted in menu for Sette of Odd Volumes dinner, 22 May 1923, at which John Lane spoke on *The Yellow Book*.[197] Other examples belonged to Clement K. Shorter, editor of *The Sphere* and *The Illustrated London News;* the design, by an unidentified artist, was possibly reproduced in one of those periodicals.

---

[193] The date appears at the foot of the spine, not on title-page.
[194] (ca. 1889–1933), British-born artist much influenced by Beardsley, who worked most of his life in Germany and was best known for his illustrations to *The Sphinx* by Oscar Wilde (1920).
[195] The text has also been attributed—with little evidence—to Ronald Firbank.
[196] Gallatin p. 139.
[197] The Sette's initials ("O. V") are found in the drawing; the menu (folded leaf) reproduces the pierrot design from invitation card for Lane's 1895 Odd Volumes "Smoke," checklist no. 83.

Index